From the Grass Roots
to Bamboo Shoots

From the Grass Roots to Bamboo Shoots

Bob Schieck

Copyright © 2015 by Bob Schieck.

Library of Congress Control Number: 2015905081
ISBN: Hardcover   978-1-5035-5913-4
                Softcover   978-1-5035-5914-1
                eBook   978-1-5035-5915-8

All rights reserved. No part of this book may be reproduced or transmitted in any form or by any means, electronic or mechanical, including photocopying, recording, or by any information storage and retrieval system, without permission in writing from the copyright owner.

Any people depicted in stock imagery provided by Thinkstock are models, and such images are being used for illustrative purposes only.
Certain stock imagery © Thinkstock.

Print information available on the last page.

Rev. date: 05/28/2015

To order additional copies of this book, contact:
Xlibris
1-888-795-4274
www.Xlibris.com
Orders@Xlibris.com
702513

Contents

About the Author vii
Prologue ix
As Preview xi
Introduction xiii
About the Book xv
Acknowledgments xvii

Chapter 1: The First Day in China................................... 1
Chapter 2: First Look: Seeing the World from
 a Different Angle 6
Chapter 3: Start to Enjoy a Different Look 12
Chapter 4: At the Bank(s)..17
Chapter 5: Looking for a Place to Live......................... 22
Chapter 6: Looking for a No. 1 Bank and Right Arm 32
Chapter 7: Chinese Dinner Is Something
 Different and Special 44
Chapter 8: The Lighter Side of Chinese Life................ 53
Chapter 9: Government from a Different Light 60
Chapter 10: A Royal Dinner and After? 71
Chapter 11: Getting the Job Search "Right"? 77
Chapter 12: Finding the "Right" House 84

Chapter 13: Meals on Wheels 92
Chapter 14: Looking for a Factory Site and School
          for the Kids Followed By a Treasure Hunt............ 98
Chapter 15: More Cultural Exposure 108
Chapter 16: Sight Seeing First Class..119
Chapter 17: For Dinner: East Meets West..............................126
Chapter 18: Finding Ms. Chu, Right-Hand Woman 131
Chapter 19: Enjoying a Real Family 147
Chapter 20: Mission Accomplished..163

About the Author

Bob Schieck has lived overseas for more than seven years, including Asia, and done business for some fifty years worldwide in four continents, working for US Corporate enterprises and in his own business. He has the experience in buying foreign businesses, setting up new businesses, and operating his own businesses.

PROLOGUE

The *Oriental* and the *Occidental* come from diverse cultural backgrounds, with many values at opposite ends of the spectrum of life. Despite these differences, which seem *poles* apart, we cannot criticize them on the basis of a mere surface assessment, but we must try to understand their logic . . . their values . . . from their point of origin . . . not ours. Hopefully, from this basis . . . a fair understanding of their culture will emerge in our thought process!? One thing is clear, the Oriental and the Occidental, both are people who have the same basic needs and wants from and for others, but show it in many different ways. Their values, *contrast* to our lifestyles, must be accepted by all of us, as we view others for what they mean to them and *not* how they appear to us. Acceptance of these differences in others—rather than concluding that *we are right* and *they're wrong*—will help to build the bridges across the *gaps* of people's languages and cultural and religious barriers to a Peaceful world.

As Preview

As we walked out of the hallowed halls of the Grand Hotel, T.C. held onto my arm and talked to me like a father, calling me by my first name, saying, "Tai Le, it is important that you understand the Yin and Yang theory because it is the main thread of our culture. The words Yin and Yang have many meanings, but for one 'Yin' definition, there is always an opposite 'Yang' meaning. For example, Yin can be interpreted to mean female. Yang, likewise, carries the meaning of male." So engrossed was he in wanting to make his explanation clear to me, we sat down in the lobby, and he pulled out a piece of paper and listed the many word definitions of both and handed the paper to me. The definitions for Yin were listed on the left and Yang on the right.

Yin	Yang
Female	Male
Negative	Positive
Moon	Sun
Earth	Heaven
Cloudy	Clear

T.C. continued, "Tai Le, I want you to understand that all the 'Yin' characters are negative. This does not mean they are bad. It takes forces from both directions to achieve the desired balance so important to our lives as we relate to politics, economics, our weather, and our relationship to others. Am I making myself clear?" Thinking to myself that the concept was so simple, I wondered how come it hadn't been expressed by our Western ancestors in such a clear picture, and I acknowledged, "T.C, it is very clear and logical, and I accept the theory completely."

"Good!" he exclaimed. As he stood up and said, "Now, let's expose you to some of our good negative forces." As we get into the car, Henry gave the driver instructions to go to CIRO's, after which he and his father proceeded to give me an explanation. "Tai Le, my father and I would like to take you to CIRO's, a well-known dance hall." T.C. then chimed in, "The good negative element in this experience is that Yin and Yang get together to dance. Again, two opposites attract to each other, for the purpose of mutual interest. The man to enjoy himself, relaxing in the company of a young attractive woman, and the woman, while pleasing the man, creates an opportunity to earn a comfortable living." Henry interjected with an explanation of the rules. "When we get there, you will have a selection of girls to choose from, or Father and I can arrange, with the manager, for a girl who speaks English for you to dance with. The girl will stay with you for three dances, and then, if you do not want her and would like to look for another partner, she is free to rotate to other tables." T.C. then counseled, saying, "If you find a girl you would like to keep as your dance partner for the evening, let me know and I'll arrange it with the manager. If you would like to take her home, later in the evening, then you will have to negotiate the arrangement on your own. If you should need translation services, Henry or I will be available on a no-fee basis, until you return to your hotel room." With a chuckle to his voice, he said, "By then, you shouldn't need any further assistance. Hao bu hao?"

INTRODUCTION

As China emerges into the twenty-first century, the rest of the world, politically and economically, is just beginning to feel the importance of understanding of this culture, both in ancient and modern-day reality. This story is intended to be written in a light vein. Humorous, I hope . . . helping the readers to better appreciate the nuances of this part of the Orient and its entry into the rest of the world. I am sure that most Chinese when reading these thoughts from the perspective of a "round eye" will not feel that we are laughing at them *or* being critical of them, their lifestyle, or their values but will laugh with the Western reader and understand that this is a story of how we see and how much we need to understand them just as they see much that is humorous in our way of life. This book is my way of saying thanks to the people of Taiwan and China, where I lived for some three and half years, as well as having done business in China now for some twenty years. It is my wish to preserve the bonds of the many wonderful friendships that have developed between *Our Grass Roots* and their *Bamboo Shoots*. Being a China watcher and a believer in peace for mankind, I only hope that the Chinese will be allowed to guide their own destiny and will not be used as a "pawn" in the great game of political *chess*, that is being played every day in every part of this world, by the *users* of the *usees*.

About the Book

Re: ABC (A Business in China) Understand that we, Americans, live in a social and business environment which has very different practices. We are now spreading our business enterprise philosophy around the world, but in order to achieve success, we need to attempt to understand that other cultures have different approaches to conducting business.

We need to go into our seeding of worldwide business with an open mind as to what are the foreign philosophy guidelines, so we can bridge these differences. Hence, the analogy, "From Our Grass Roots" to their "Bamboo Shoots."

Footnote:
Some of our readers will be aware of some apparent discrepancies; with descriptions of city and country locations that appear to be in error; China versus Taiwan. And also as to the identification of monies as being incorrect values and labels. The author has lived in and/or worked in both countries; he is bringing these experiences together knowingly.

Acknowledgments

To the three most important *women* in a businessman's (Occidental) life . . .

- My wife Judy who has been my inspiration now for some fifty years.
- My mother Lois by whom I was nurtured and whose constant praise got me to manhood.
- My office administrators: Rita, Jane, Marilyn, Donna, Tamlin, Arlona, and Dee, all of whom have been a part of this story and/or typed and edited the transcript.

Note: If I were an Oriental businessman, I would have had to add perhaps two more categories of women to my life in my credits.

Concubine(s) . . . now legally illegal . . . isn't everything that is fun?

Playgirl(s) . . . legal, but very expensive . . . isn't everything that is fun?

CHAPTER 1

The First Day in China

At a traditional round restaurant table, with seven other Chinese businessmen, enjoying a twelve-course Chinese meal, I finally had the courage to ask my Chinese host, "What is this thing that looks like a freshly cut wood chip?" Tien Lai (*A member of the Chinese ministry of commerce, who was assigned to our USA parent company to be our host in the process of setting up ABC, A Business in China*), my host and Chinese Government Host, replied, "That's a bamboo shoot. All that is life in China stems from the bamboo tree shoots."

Upon finishing one of the world's greatest culinary pleasures, a Chinese meal, I put down those instruments of Western frustration, the chopsticks, and wondered what other pleasures for the late evening Tien Lai, as a most gracious Chinese host (on my first day in this new country for me, but the oldest country civilization), had in store for me.

As we wiped our hands on the perfume-scented towels, I realized it was late and the day had been a long one. I started my departure earlier in the day from Tokyo by air and was still recovering from jet lag from the fourteen hours flight from the USA. I longed for a bed, which right now would have felt like one of the world's seven pleasures. However, Tien Lai had other plans, and as eager in social plans as in business, he said, "Tai Le (to be my new Chinese name, with as close a sounding as my given English name, *Tyler*), you need best Chinese dessert, so we go to other restaurant, HAO BU HAO (meaning OK)?" Quietly, the six office underlings of Tien Lai excused themselves and went in other directions, presumably home to their wives?

However, sleep was not what my host had in mind and so came the next lesson in Chinese philosophy, centuries old, that of Yin and Yang. That is in every action and reaction in life, we have some *good* to balance out the *bad*. So, the weariness of sleep in my mind needed in Tien Lai's mind to have some anti-sleep stimulus. In the taxi, on our way across town, through streets and alleys teeming with people at 10:00 in the evening, dodging bicycles and carts, Tien Lai started a philosophical conversation with a series of questions, the significance of which I did not fully realize until some months later, struggling with a language tutor, to learn the basics of the Chinese language, Chung Kuo Hwa. "Tai Le, how long you plan to stay in my country? You bring your family? You like to learn speak our language?" I replied, "Yes, I would very much like to speak the language, and I hope that three or more years here would give me time to learn and use the language in my daily business conversations, and yes, I plan to bring my wife and three children soon." To which he then summarized, "Then, you not learn to speak Chinese well." He left it at that for me to think about his observation.

With face aglow, at my response, he said, "Tai hao le (which I will later learn it means in English, very good). Now, you have second lesson in Chinese," which I thought meant that we were going to practice a scholarly introduction to Chinese but really meant something else. As the harrowing taxi ride came to a halt and we got out of the cab, we walked up a flight of stairs to a second level to open the door to another cultural event . . . the *girlie* restaurant. Tien Lai said to the lady greeting us at the door, "Mama San, we need special room. Hao bu hao (another Yin and Yang axiom, literally translated, *good* or *bad*)?"

So, we were ushered into a special dining room, with the familiar round table, but with unfamiliar accomplices: four beautiful Chinese girls dressed in their traditional Chinese Chi Pao gowns, with slits up the side to show a lot of leg and tight-fitting bodice to show off the rest of their slender and curvaceous bodies. Now, don't get me wrong. These girls of twenty to twenty-five years of age were not painted ladies looking like a bunch of prostitutes. Each looked demure and shy and very attractive, like you would imagine the "Chinese girl next door" that you would want your son to meet and bring home. However, the thought raced thru my mind, "I am sure my wife and Tien Lai's wife(s) would think otherwise, so . . ."

After the introductions in Chinese, Mama San left the room, saying, "You be good. I leave you. Have fun. Hao bu hao?" Tien Lai proceeded like he had had prior experience in this situation, and I am sure he had. As the six of us took seats, two girls on each side of us, a most beautiful tray of fresh fruits was placed in the center of the round table. Tien Lai, as the master of ceremonies, took immediate control, and although not a tall man, of average height for a Chinese man, five foot five inches, his enthusiasm and his obvious role as favored customer gave him a "ten feet tall" stature. The girls immediately recognized Tien Lai, and judging from the fuss they made over him, it was obvious that he was ranked as being a most attractive and desirable mate for the night. He introduced them in their Chinese names as "Lotus Blossom, Moon, Butterfly, and Angel," and they promptly blushed. It was apparent that they were not truly accustomed to me as a Westerner (round eye) in their midst. So, that made everyone except Tien Lai somewhat bashful about the situation, just to begin.

Moon and Butterfly began the cultural lesson by alternately feeding me the most succulent pieces of fresh fruit, pineapple, watermelon, star fruit, apples, and Japanese apple/pears, and filling of my glass with a potent liquor, Shiao Shing, which is the equivalent of Chinese "white" lightning, 80 percent alcohol made from sorghum.

Needless to say, I was overwhelmed with the feast and the toasting process. Tien Lai said, "Tai Le Hsien Sheng (Mr. Tai Le, in a more formal address), you need someone like Moon and Butterfly to learn you to speak Chinese, OK?" Seeing my awkwardness, he repeated to both girls in Chinese, and their faces reflected an immediate acknowledgment of this command and need. They smiled, and then Moon spoke softly in Mandarin (Chinese), "Waw shr Nide Lao Shr, hao bu hao?" To which Tien Lai said to me, "Moon would like to be your Chinese teacher, OK?" How does one say no to such a question, but wanting to learn, I nodded and said, "Yes" with somewhat of a crimson blush.

Now, Tien Lai interjected, saying, "Tai Le, language school is fine, but if you really like speak Chinese, you must have someone like Moon or Butterfly to live with you." Considering this option caused my further embarrassment and reddishness and tittering of all four of the girls. My imagination raced as thoughts conjured up in my mind like, "Great! He's right, and think of all of the side benefits that would go along with that proposition." Then with a clear Western conscience, as a husband and father, I quickly came to my senses, with instant answers like,

Question: Could I live with one of them? Only to answer, No, my wife does a bed check every night.

Question: Could I pass either of them off as a maid for the house? No, my wife will insist on hiring of the help.

Question: Could I really afford to have a mistress? No, it is not a socially acceptable Western custom, let alone the cost . . .

And most importantly, even if I could, in good faith, answer *yes* to any one of the questions, then could I, as an Occidental, and a WASP, by cultural background, live with my conscience? Unhappily, but relieved, I knew that without any doubt, the unequivocal answers were *no*.

As the evening progressed, the girls introduced me to my first Chinese social lessons:

1. How to Gampai (chug-a-lug) or Sui E (sip as you like) and 2. polite language phrases. As *king* for my first night in China, I was really enjoying the feast: eating, drinking, playing Chinese parlor games, and talking about moving back to the hotel to sleep or bed elsewhere? Tien Lai asked the leading question, "Which of these two ladies you want to go home with?" Doing a

practiced yawn and an apology for being tired, and embarrassed, that I did not want to hurt any feelings of my host and the girls, I clumsily tripped over excuses, saying, "I'd like to take both of them home, but I really need to catch up on some uninterrupted shut-eye and go back to the hotel alone. Maybe another night, when I catch up on my nights and days, OK?"

Since such special tender loving care and attention had been devoted to me, as the guest, I fully expected my excuses to be met with disappointment by my host and the girls . . . but I hoped, not with hard feelings. Instead, my excuses were accepted graciously and with a promise of *next time* . . . when I was feeling rested, the same offer would be extended.

Back to the hotel, in a taxi alone and feeling a little cheated, while my host, Tien Lai, accepted the invitation of Lotus Blossom, I came to my first understanding and deep appreciation that there are some fundamental and true social custom differences between the East and the West.

Chapter 2

First Look: Seeing the World from a Different Angle

Awakening to a bright and sunny second day, I silently reflected on my first day, saying to myself, "Wow! If today and every day in China is going to be like yesterday, this China life is going to be a fascinating experience." However, in the very next instant, I came to the realization that a lot of these types of experiences were going to be most difficult to explain to his American-based company and boss (the President—International) and more importantly, to not only my wife but also to my children, but explain, I *must*. Then, the questions continued in my mind, *How?*" "There ain't *any* way to explain some of the facts. This was a whole new way of life, and you've got to be there and see it, feel it, to believe it."

Coming back from this reverie, I remembered that that day, I had an appointment with my Chinese legal firm, so I quickly shaved, showered, dressed, and left the room for breakfast in the hotel. The First Hotel provided a first-class pseudo-Western environment, so for the moment, I did not feel dis-Oriented. (Ever wonder where that term came from?) However, upon walking out the front door of the hotel, into another world, a re-Orientation process came into play. At the hotel curbside was a tiny cab, built for people of Asian stature, and I proceeded to bump the frame with my head, knees, and brief case, all in successive movements.

I looked at the driver and instructed in English, "Take me, please, to Zhong Shan Road, Section 2." The driver turned around and replied, in Chinese, "Zai Nali" (translation—I don't know), at which instant, I concluded it meant that if I didn't speak any Chinese, I wasn't going to get anywhere that day. So, I reversed the process, bumping my knees and head in exiting the cab, to find the doorman to explain to the driver as to where he needed to go. You guessed right, he didn't speak enough English either, so he asked some of the other cab drivers if they could speak English, and if so, take me as their fare to my ultimate destination. Pretty soon, we had a crowd of some ten Chinese people surrounding me at the cabstand, all curious as to what was going on and all wanting to be the person who could assist in this impasse of communications. After five minutes of hand-waving and lots of loud conversation, I finally gave up on the outside scene and, somewhat frustrated and embarrassed, went back into the hotel, to the Registration desk, to see if I could find someone to help me explain to everyone where I needed to go. Grace Chen, by name . . . as calm as can be . . . and also as demurely shy and beautiful as a Chinese doll, said so politely, "Mister Tai Le, how I help?" I explained, "I would like to go to my lawyer's offices, but no one understands my English." Grace quickly volunteered, "How about I write out the address in Chinese on a piece of paper, so you can hand to driver?" "Perfect," I replied. Then, she continued, "Then, Mr. Tyler, you take hotel business card, which is Chinese. You give to driver to come back to hotel when finished. Hau bu hao?" Having learned from Moon the night before that *hao bu hao* was also their way of saying literally "do you understand?" and at the same time, "good or bad" or "OK or Not OK," and after this brief lesson in the need to prepare before going out into the Chinese real world, I responded to Grace by saying, "Hao," and wandered back out to start over again, some ten minutes later, to find a taxi. Careful not to bump my head, knees, etc. again, I got into another cab and handed the driver the note prepared by Grace, and we headed on our way.

Looking at my watch, I now realized that I was going to be at least fifteen minutes late but much wiser in the ways of a

"Westerner" in China, in the future. Like a Boy Scout, one should always "Be Prepared," and above all else, "exercise Oriental Patience," or the Buddhist philosophy, "always be calm." I proudly handed the driver the card written in Chinese characters, and he nodded, simply, and drove on.

Settled in, I took my first opportunity to look around in the broad daylight and realized that the taxi driver must have had lessons as a Kamikaze Pilot, because he was already with reckless abandon, weaving in and out of the narrow one and half lane traffic. At this moment, I did not know how I was going to tell "U-Turn Charlie" how to slow down . . . to tell him "that I want to get to the lawyer's office alive." So, instead of looking straight ahead at the road, full of bicycles and people, I looked out to the sides, trying to regain composure, and suddenly realized that I must be in the "Bar" district, which obviously surrounded the hotel, and found myself looking at many miniskirts. These lean, thin-legged creatures, with too much makeup were almost as unnerving as "Charlie's" driving skills. Now, I began to appreciate what I had heard: it pays to be "A China Watcher."

I remembered that my wife and I had been asked to be "China Watchers" by several of the local Hometown USA organizations, including the Church and the League of Women Voters, and to report our observations. I quickly vowed, then and there, that I'd do my share of the *watching*," but probably could not vouch for the propriety of my reports, especially if asked to give them in person.

At that time, I decided that I'd better concentrate on the meeting to come in a few minutes, with the Chinese lawyers, as the taxi pulled up to the entrance of this third floor office over the Bank of China, in the financial district of this major metropolis. I attempted to pay the driver, with some leftover Yen acquired in Tokyo, several days earlier . . . with the driver shaking his head and saying in Chinese, "Bu hao," which was quickly translated as "no good." Finally, the fare was settled with a bill that had the numerals of RMB$50 on it, and when the driver gratefully nodded his acceptance, I knew I had overpaid. In the process of exiting the taxi, I forgot the routine of how to extract this larger than Chinese body out of the small taxi, so, proceeded, again, to bump my head and my knees and get my briefcase caught in the door before stepping out to the sidewalk and straightening up.

Ascending the stairs, I began to try to focus on the task ahead to start a foreign invested firm in China, ABC Ltd., (*A Business in China*), which was to be a subsidiary of a US Electronics firm 'at the grass roots', or was it to be a "bamboo shoots" plan? After a brief round of introductions to get acquainted with this father-son firm, T.C. Chao and son, Henry (his young Yale Law School associate), all three of us were soon engrossed in the legal web of foreign investment regulations, host provincial laws and guidelines, registration procedures, and legal "chops" (rubber stamp—Chinese characters) which are the same as an official signature in China. As my mind was swimming in legality, tea was served. Chinese tea (unlike the Japanese Green Tea, which is somewhat bitter, and which, like a martini, takes some repetitious cultivation to appreciate) is excellent and comes in numerous flavors and is most enjoyable *except* for one most disconcerting feature: the tea leaves which float at the top get into your mouth, unless strained by sifting thru your teeth, making it extremely difficult to enunciate when drinking and talking. I quickly realized that it would take some practice for me to achieve the art of drinking Chinese tea, but in the meantime, be viewed as a Western barbarian, who would spit the leaves back into the glass or extract the leaves with his fingers from his lips. Needless to say, I felt that I was leaving a less than cultured opinion of myself and my manners with my hosts, the Chaos.

Well, after several hours of intense conversations, we finally navigated around to the subject of a specific legal fee for their services for the ABC's Ltd. legal set-up, and suffice it to say, their legal services did not carry the connotation of being "cheap labor," that most foreign investors are usually accused of exploiting. I could only surmise that Henry's training at Yale Law School also included a course in "Fee Schedules" with the USA rates.

Feeling, at this point, a little bit uncomfortable, with this most uncomfortable monetary issue, and last night's *White Lightning* coming around to taunt the head, I said, "Excuse me, T.C. and Henry, I have a splitting headache coming on. Perhaps, you might have a couple of aspirin in the office?" Lao Chao (Lao, the term used by others to show respect for elders, meaning *old*) hearing this request, immediately interjected to say, "Could I prescribe a Chinese remedy to relieve the pain?" Not wanting to show any cowardice at acceptance of Chinese ways, I replied, "Please, Mr. Chao, I'll try anything, once." So, T.C. gave the thumps-up signal and said, "Tai Le Hsien Sheng, I guarantee that the pain will be gone within five to ten minutes and you'll feel like a new man." Proudly, T.C. had their Tea Lady bring in a little square package, with a golden dragon on the front and lots of Chinese characters on the back, and proceeded to open the package, took my open hand, poured the powder contents in my hand, and instructed, "Now, pour the powder into the glass of warm water and drink slowly." T.C. continued to explain, "This and many other Chinese herbal medicines are the reasons for my eighty years of good health, keen mind, and manly virility." By the time T.C. had finished his campaign speech for pharmacology, I felt relief from the oncoming headache and within the prescribed five minutes, had completely shaken off the throbbing, with a clear mind. Looking at T.C. and Henry, I said, "I am a true believer and am eagerly willing to try some more of your prescriptions for life."

As they finished the business agenda, Henry extended a business handshake and said, "Do you have anything planned for this evening? My Father and I would like to introduce you to some fine Chinese cuisine, the best of our seafood, in the art of Chinese cooking, and then some Chinese culture, after. Hao bu hao?" Having previously made a commitment for dinner, with the US banking firm, Chase Manhattan, I regretfully expressed my apologies and asked courteously, "May I ask for a rain check?" Thinking that this idiom perhaps would not be understood in Chinese, T.C. took the liberty to explain only to find that this saying also dates back some centuries in Chinese philosophy. "The sage," T.C. quipped, "I think that this is old custom of China that Marco Polo brought back to Italy, after his travels in China." Right then, I acknowledged to both of the Chaos',

"You win." I came to the silent conclusion that the Chinese do know how to engage the Occidental in "one-up's man ship." Not allowing the offer of an evening out to be an "open" matter, T.C. then extended his offer for a night on the town to the following evening, and, of course, I accepted and bowed to both of the Chaos on my way out to say "*good-bye*." Waiting to have the last word, T.C. replied, "Dzai Jen, Tai Le Hsien Sheng," and explained that *Dzai Jen*, in Chinese, means "see you again" to which he explained, "We never say Good-bye. That is too final."

Chapter 3

Start to Enjoy a Different Look

Looking at my watch, the next morning at 11:15 a.m., I noticed that I was probably going to be late for my 11:30 a.m. appointment with the US (Foreign) bank, the Bank of International Commerce (BIC), that was on tap to be our liaison with corporate headquarters back home, so as I left the hotel entrance, I hustled to the curbside to hail a cab. At least four or more responded. One did a U-turn right there in the street. Quickly selecting the one who made the safest curbside approach, I looked around to see if I would be verbally accused of playing favoritism, but the others went off, on the prowl, again, without so much as an angry glance or a word. Imagine that civil reaction in New York City?

I executed my entry into this cab masterfully and almost convinced myself, mentally, that I was going to, for the first time, enjoy this ride. As I got situated, however, I felt somewhat cramped. As I leaned over to give the cab driver directions, I began to understand why. He was a hefty three hundred pounds, who looked like the proverbial Sumo wrestler with clothes on. He had pushed his seat back as far as it would go, causing my knees to be jackknifed and virtually pinned to my chest. Oh well!

This time, having thought about my destination in advance, I handed the driver a letter with the Chinese characters on the BIC stationary, so, instantly, his face beamed, indicating his familiarity with the location of the bank. I braced myself, as he made a quick start, darting out of the slow lane, to the middle of the road, dodging the bicycles, carts, and double-parked cars. The density of people, the overwhelming numbers of cars, and the closeness to the sidewalk and buildings left me with the feeling that the world had accelerated to twice its normal pace. Looking ahead about one block, I spotted a green light at the next intersection, and then instantly, the cab veered to his left, occupying the oncoming vehicle lane to make just a left-hand turn, and then an abrupt U-turn into two lanes of opposing traffic. Amidst an echo of honking cars, we sped off unscratched, in the opposite direction.

As we got closer to the downtown area, the traffic became more congested; we got boxed into our own lanes of traffic and the safety factor of being an occupant, without control, improved. On our way, I spotted a major bus terminal, swarming with people, recognizing it as a major hub of transportation and then shortly, what appeared to be the major railway station. Despite the lack of road disciplines, I noticed in both locations an interesting paradox. Long queues of people were lined up in a very orderly and patient manner, waiting to board these buses and trains, with no signs of pushing and shoving. Strange, given the obvious rules of the highway!

Dead ahead of us was my first glimpse of a Chinese gate which we have seen in the movies, as a rampart of a walled city. It was an ominous structure of ancient Chinese architecture. Now, I was seeing a true part of both ancient and modern history such that I knew for certain that I was really in China. Just about as quickly as I was becoming a student of history, I became oriented to the fact that the car was now going in circles. Entering into a traffic round-about circle is another unforgettable driving experience, reminding one of playing a game of roulette in your car. The roulette is a 360-degree interchange, with four to six entry and exit points designed to eliminate intersections. I wasn't quite sure what we were going to do, but after getting stuck in the inside lane and going around three times, the driver finally managed to navigate out of the pack and had us pointed in a 180-degree opposite direction. Within one minute of that experience, he pulled up in front of our destination, the BIC bank. Paying the RenMinBi number on the meter, fifteen, amounted to a $1.95 total, definitely cheaper than the entry fee to one of our roller-coaster amusement parks and still in one piece, I found that I had experienced a lifetime of thrills, in only ten minutes.

Within minutes of my entry into the lobby of BIC, I was being escorted to the spacious and handsomely decorated wood panels into the offices of Barry Frazier, managing director of the bank. As I attempted to apologize for my lateness, Barry countered, saying, "Don't worry about it. You couldn't have been more 'on time.' Being late is a Chinese custom, intended to establish a caller's importance. As a Managing Director of your new Chinese-company-to-be, you're entitled to be as much as thirty minutes late to your appointments, unless you are calling on a person of higher political or business station." After having a good laugh at my unplanned "luck," we sat down to get better acquainted, both as to business as well as socially. Within minutes, I could tell that I was going to like Barry. He was straight forward in his manner, and being an eight-year veteran of the Asian business world, he certainly knew his way around. After enjoying a real cup of coffee and making a complete round of introductions with his managerial staff, Barry suggested that we go around the corner for lunch at the China Hotel.

I soon found out that a Chinese lunch is not the quick bite: sandwich and soup with a cup of coffee or brew routine that we Westerners are willing to accept. Although the meal was not nearly as elaborate as the twelve-course feast the night before, it was a casual six-course affair that took the better part of an hour and a half to accomplish. Now, don't get me wrong. I thoroughly enjoyed the meal and the company, but I began to feel uncomfortable after the first thirty minutes, like maybe I was cheating the company by taking such a long lunch hour again. Barry attempted to put me at ease explaining, "One and a half hours for lunch is not unusual for Chinese businessmen. They make up for that grace by working much later in the evening, and also, their work week calls for a six-day routine, rather than our usual five days"

The course of conversation centered pretty much on the living, schooling, and social climates for any expatriate living in China. Of course, this was going to be an area in which I was fully conversant, upon my return home, to discuss with my family. I must have fired a hundred questions at Barry, all of which he patiently and thoroughly answered and then summarized by volunteering to supply me with several books and pamphlets, specifically written by expatriates to answer and allay the fears of the neophyte family preparing to move to China. He said, "When we get back to the office, I'll arm you with the book *Living in China* by the wife of my predecessor and a pamphlet by the American Chamber of Commerce. Further, I've arranged to have you meet on the weekend a couple of reputable realtors to show you some community living places around the city. Take your camera with so you can show the family some of these typical residential areas."

Slowly, but surely, I came to the realization that the relationship being established at this lunch was becoming more than that of just a client-banker; a feeling of fraternity became evident. Several important object lessons also came into our discussions, as Barry emphasized, "Tai Le, there are two different lifestyles here in the Orient, and specifically, China. You'll have to choose in your mind very soon as to which role you want to play. If you want to be a Playboy, the business-social and social-social circuit can be yours on a thirty-day per month schedule. On the other hand, if you want to maintain a happy family life, keep your wife and kids involved. Sacrifice the nightlife Playboy routine and settle for maybe an occasional night out with the boys.

"One more important point. Don't come to live overseas unless your wife is excited about the living prospects and is an adventurer and she is willing to accept a few hardships. Wives who can't wait to go back home can be one of any businessman's biggest liabilities and a wet blanket to a great family experience."

To that I responded, "Barry, my wife and I lived in Japan for three years when we were first married and had two kids there, so I think we are ready."

"Well, enough said. How about getting back to the business of work?" he remarked.

With a pleasant feeling of being sated with food and amply endowed with social awareness, we left the restaurant and returned to the office to resume business conversations, and I had a feeling of great inner satisfaction that going from the "Grass Roots to the Bamboo Shoots" was going to turn out well.

Chapter 4

At the Bank(s)

"Banking in China is unlike any other financial experience you've had in the United States," explained Barry as he proceeded to outline the rules under which the game is played. "CIBC is a foreign-owned financial institution," he said, "and is restricted to providing services related to the financial settlement of funds related to foreign exchange. We're not allowed to provide the normal services of maintaining bank checking and deposit accounts for our clients. In other words, we can finance all of your investment capital and export-import fund needs, but we can't manage your local cash transactions. The Central Bank of China limits our activities and restricts us from maintaining branch offices. So, you'll have to establish a banking relationship with one of the local banks, almost all of which are partially owned by the government."

"Barry," I asked, "what if I want to maintain a personal bank account?" To which he replied, "You guessed it . . . see your friendly Chinese bankers. Don't be concerned though. You'll find the Chinese to be very shrewd money people. In fact, I'll be happy to recommend two or more of the banks that I think are the best and help make appointments to talk to them about establishing your relationships." With a nod on my part, Barry instructed his secretary to contact the president of both the Tenth Commercial and the Tai Fong Banks for appointments the following day. Within minutes, that mission was accomplished, and Barry had switched the conversation to another topic—the Chinese businessman.

The minutes and hours slipped by rapidly, and Barry recapped his observations of the day by saying, "The Chinese businessman is a real entrepreneur. You look at any major city in Asia and you find a Chinese business community. Hell, in many countries, they control the economy. I guess I'd consider the Chinese, along with the Jewish, as being the two best ethnic group merchants in the world.

"Chinese businessmen will work from dawn until past dusk, and when they don't work, they play. I'd consider them to be among the world's best family men, but yet they seem to find the time to play their extracurricular social games, from golf to girls . . . from bar to bed. You know, stop to think of it, I don't know when they find time to sleep!"

After telling Barry of my experience at the girlie restaurant, he said, "Tai Le, you've just been introduced to the elementary level of social school. Wait 'til you get a chance to do some graduate work on your Master's in Human Engineering."

With a few "touch" gestures of his hands and his personal chuckle, he changed the subject asking, "Have you any 'druthers' on where we eat tonight?" Without allowing time for an answer, he said, "Have you been to the 'O' Club yet?" With a quick response to my "No, I haven't," he was on the phone. "Ron, how'd you and Penny like to join Kathy and me at the *'O' Club* tonight? I need to salvage one sane night for Mr. Tai Le. Remember, he's from ABC Electronics . . . while he's here in Shenzhen this next week . . . Great, we'll meet you there about 7:30."

Next he was on the phone to his wife saying, "Kathy, can you feed the children early and be ready when I come home about 6:30 to have a couple of goodies and drinks with Mr. Tai Le? Remember, I mentioned he'd be in town? Let's go to the *American Club* then for some Surf 'n Turf."

As he hung up, he buzzed his secretary who brought in a stack of papers and letters for his signature along with his daily mail. After a ten-minute signature and "chop" session, he piled all the mail in his briefcase and explained as we headed for the door, "Tai Le, do you know what the 'chop' is for? Well, the 'chop' is a legal stamp that's just like your signature on a Chinese document. Hand-carved, each is one of a kind. You're legally liable for any actions which involve the use of your 'chop.' Make sure you use it only when you know and understand what is being chopped." With that final piece of advice, my business orientation for the day came to a close.

Barry and I got into his car, which his chauffeur had brought to the front door. After introducing me to his driver, George, we took off for the *President Hotel* and the first safe and sane ride I'd had since coming to Shenzhen.

In between social conversation about our mutual golf and tennis interests, I interjected a question about the driving disciplines. "Barry, do the natives all drive like these kamikaze taxi drivers?" He laughed and said, "Yes, and as soon as you get behind the wheel, you'll be using the same tactics. The art of driving here is like a game of chicken. Your horn and nerve will determine how well you'll get around." Then, in a more serious mood, he said, "Tai Le, just remember, the motor vehicle conveyance was almost non-existent here ten to fifteen years ago. Then, one day, the fathers of wisdom got the bright idea that the car could replace the pedicab and overnight, these former bicycle peddlers were behind the wheel. Hell, it'll take a generation to develop a consciousness in the people that a car is a lethal weapon, not just a faster pedicab.

"Another thing, watch out for people who dart out into the streets, almost as if they dare the cars to hit them. They didn't have parents telling them as children to stop-look-listen before crossing the street. It's just going to take time to develop these safety habits. I figure that if they learned to queue up for buses and trains in an orderly manner, which they have, then they'll learn how to be courageous and careful drivers in time."

About this time, we turned the corner to the *President* Hotel to find ourselves caught in a wild, horn-honking, every lane is my lane traffic jam. George turned to us and said, "Mr. Frazier, maybe it take two generations!" As we all finished laughing, George finally made it to the front door.

As I got out, I said, "Barry, how about relieving some of the traffic tensions and come on up to the room for a quick Scotch!" So, we both wound our way through the crowded lobby. It looked like a tour group was just arriving or ready to depart. As I approached the desk, Patty Chen looked over to me and smiled asking, "How did your day go?" "Ding Hao," I replied to convey the impression that it was "very good," and then we turned for the elevator.

With a quick shave, a fresh shirt, and a Scotch and water, we headed back downstairs for the car. As we got on the elevator, I became conscious of a rather distinguished-looking Chinese gentleman talking with a very beautiful young girl. Both were well dressed, and I thought to myself, "He sure has a very lovely daughter," and at that, we were exiting from the elevator and out through the lobby looking for George and the car.

As we got back into the car, Barry grinned and said, "You'll have to get used to many of those quick-change and turnaround schedules." We snaked our way through the heavy, rush-hour traffic and finally out onto a dual lane highway and quickly George was doing 50 MPH. Barry said, "How do you like this? It's the only expressway in China—all three miles of it." As quickly as we got on to it, we had to get off and then back onto the crowded streets of another village. "This is *Peitou*, where the Fraziers live." "You mean," I asked almost with embarrassment, "the same one as the *Newsweek* article with the picture of the G.I. in the hot bath?" "Yup," he chucked, "and if you plan to live here, be prepared to raise some suspicious eyebrows at the corporate offices when they hear about it." Barry queried, "Have you ever heard the background on the infamous *Peitou*?" Without waiting for an answer, he continued, "The Japanese, when they invaded China, set up this area as their 'heaven on earth.' During the war, they brought all the kamikaze pilots here one week before their flights to let them taste the fruit and honey of life before they were sent off on their last mission. The sulfur baths, because of health reasons, and the girls who are an indispensable part of bathing, continued after the war to perform their healing miracles, and now once again Peitou is almost a mecca to the Japanese businessman and tourist." Pausing, he said wryly, "Even a few Mei Kuo Ren (as we Americans are called) feel that the place has the powers to heal." Chuckling as we pulled up the drive to his house, "You'll probably have a chance to test the faith, one of these days."

Chapter 5

Looking for a Place to Live

While we drove up the main street of Peitou, I caught quick glimpses of the people, the shops, plenty of motorcycles, and a quiet park in the center of town. Then we began to drive into a narrow lane with very secluded residential homes built behind walls. I found myself in a somewhat tranquil state, enjoying my surroundings, knowing that I could find happiness here in this country.

As we proceeded to make a left turn into a stately driveway, my reverie was broken as I watched a motorcycle come darting out of a nearby alleyway, with a pretty, shapely girl sitting side-saddle on the back. I had to take a 180-degree look, because she was not only sitting there nonchalantly reading a book, but with her legs crossed, and there sure was a lot of thigh showing. My mind's image pictured her as the young man's sister studying for a final exam on her way to school, when Barry interrupted, saying, "Well, here we are." He smiled wryly and asked, "What'd you think of the maiden on the motorcycle?" To which I answered, "Nice, but I wonder if she is an A-student." Bursting out in laughter, he shattered my whole mental image when he said, "She's no student, but she's one hell of a teacher! Conducts one of the best sex education programs in Peitou." Still chuckling, he said, "Let me explain over a drink. Come on in." I looked around before we entered the house to find ourselves situated in the midst of a garden sanctuary. Within the four walls, Barry's place offered a beautifully landscaped lawn. It looked like the No. 9 green at the country club back home with an abundance of bushes, lovely sculptured pines, with hundreds of beautiful blossoming flowers, and in the center of all this grace was a nice-sized swimming pool accompanied by a Chinese-styled gazebo. The splendor of the outdoors was quickly matched by the pleasing simplicity of the interior décor of their very comfortable home. As we entered the front door, Barry was greeted with a nice homecoming kiss and . . . I, almost at the same instant, found myself becoming homesick for my wife and family, was introduced to Kathy with a most gracious handshake.

I'm not sure which was most captivating, Kathy or the house. She looked the perfect lady, tastefully dressed in a white blouse and a black, full-length evening skirt with a single strand of pearls around her neck which drew attention to her smooth, creamy-white skin. Her soft black hair was long, swept to one side, and it accentuated her lovely face. "Tai Le," she said, "let me show you around the house while Barry fixes us a drink."

The layout of the house was centered around an atrium, done in Oriental style with a rock garden, a few bonsai trees, and again, the ever-present flower blossoms. When the weather was nice, the atrium could be opened to the living room, dining room, and a family room. Kind of like outdoor living, inside. We didn't invade the privacy of the upstairs bedrooms, but Kathy didn't miss any of the details, explaining, "The upstairs layout provides four nice-size bedrooms and a game room." As we walked in the direction of the bar where Barry was busy mixing up a couple of scotch and waters and one martini for Kathy, she proceeded to give me the pros and cons of living in China and Peitou. Comments like "Chinese food is the world's greatest . . . the international schools are excellent . . . the ocean is only a thirty-minute drive . . . the mountains are as our beautiful Amahs (our maids)," she explained, "who are a Godsend, but I can't say much for the traffic, and occasionally, our neighborhood gets rather noisy." Her last comment was picked up by Barry who said, "Remember what I said about the teacher on the motorbike?"

Handing me a drink, he motioned for me to follow him, and we immediately proceeded to walk up the stairs and then on through the game room, where he opened the sliding glass door which opened out onto a balcony on the back side of the house. By now, darkness was settling in, and it was easy to look into the house immediately behind the Fraziers and see into what looked to be a dining room. Seated around a typical Chinese round table was a group of men with a female conveniently located between each. Barry said, "That's Teacher's place, and school's in session." As we watched them eating, drinking, and playing social games, the memory of my first night at the girlie restaurant was quickly recalled. Barry explained, "With our open-window air-conditioning systems, the later the evening, the more enjoyment and the louder the guests become, particularly when they are Japanese. Man, their philosophy is when you work, work hard. When you play, you play the same way you work." He went on, saying, "On the first floor sublevel are the supper baths and massage rooms. Now, on the second floor are the exercise and rest rooms." Chuckling, he added, "Not defined in the same context as we would use the words."

As we proceeded to return downstairs to the bar area, Barry continued to elaborate. "Now, Peitou has something for everyone. Hotels, restaurants, etc. Chinese style and Japanese style, but no Dairy Queen. There is no discrimination, except they don't let many, in fact . . . not *any* wives in. For that fact, there are probably quite a few husbands who can't get in at home after a night out in Peitou." Kathy even responded with a laugh on that one, and then it was time to go.

Now, as George chauffeured us back toward the hotel, I was much more conscious of the motorcycles with their precious cargo. In fact, I even saw one setup on a bicycle, and when I asked the Fraziers if that's where the phrase of "flesh-peddling" came from, everyone including George cracked up with laughter. As we passed a very nice dress shop, which Barry called to my attention, he explained, "That Madame's Boutique is GHQ for the companionship marketplace. If a hotel, bar, or otherwise hasn't got what you want, they call the dress shop with the size, name, and/or price specifications, and by shuffling the playing cards, the match is made, the books are balanced, and the motorcycle dispatched to pick up and deliver. Twenty-four-hour service is available, which is better than you can say for China Petroleum's gas station service."

Within five minutes, we pulled up into the main entrance of the 'O' Club, which I recognized to be on the main street, Chung Shan North Road, and only about a five-minute walk from the President Hotel and about the same distance in the opposite direction from the famous Grand Hotel. As the car proceeded into a driveway, flanked with towering royal palm trees, I had the feeling that we were somewhere in Miami Beach. As we stepped out of the car, under a canopy entranceway, I noticed a swimming pool complex off to the side, well populated with teenagers, all of whom seemed to be having a good time. Barry mentioned as we went in through the automatic doors into the lobby area, "Next time we have a chance to go out for dinner, remind me to take you over to the American Club, just across the road, which has a similar layout, but in addition has a couple of nice tennis courts."

We were met in the lobby by the Thackers. Ron introduced his vivacious companion, Penelope, who said, "If you ever call me that, you're on my list. Hi! I'm Penny." A bright, shiny, new personality she was. Ron and Penny were probably in their late 20s, very friendly and outgoing, a characteristic personality trait of the Midwest where they came from. Ron was a handsome, well-built guy with blond curly hair who looked like he had played fullback at one of the Big Ten schools, and Penny . . . well, she was tall, very shapely, blonde hair, blue eyes, and could well have been taken for a model in her obviously hand-crafted, form-fitting dinner dress in my favorite color, olive green.

After the brief round of introductions, we took a table in the cocktail lounge, while Barry went off to the dining room to check on the table reservations. Two drinks and much social conversation later, we were told by our dining room waitress-to-be that our table was ready. On the way, Barry announced that tonight the club had the Mongolian barbecue special, mentioning to me that he'd explain at the table all about this new experience in teasing your taste buds. As we walked into the dining area with our petite and charming waitress, Li Li, my attention was drawn to two sounds. The familiar one from inside the dining room was that of a smooth dance band and the strange ones from behind me were the click, click sounds of money going in and not nearly as much coming out of slot machines.

As we sat down, and Barry ordered one more round of drinks, I glanced around. The dining room was good size, probably seated four hundred, and was nicely decorated. The lights were low, the place was crowded, and a few couples were out on the dance floor dancing to the strains of "Jean, Jean" being vocalized by a black-haired, shapely singer in a Chinese red, sexy, low-cut, sequined evening gown. The only thing that made this place stand out as being something other than the supper club at Caesar's Place in Las Vegas was the presence of so many men in military uniforms.

Penny on my left, whom I felt most fortunate to be sitting next to, leaned over and said, "Tai Le, don't make any decisions from the menu until after I've had a chance to show you the Mongolian barbecue. It's really great, and all you can eat." I guessed I must have nearly dropped my eyeballs when I took my first look at the menu. Not only was the selection great, but the prices were fantastic. Blurting out my surprise, such that I gained attention from four tables away, I exclaimed, "God, I can't remember the last time I got a New York cut sirloin steak for US $12.75, except at the Ponderosa." Barry leaned over and said, "Partner, just one of the few limited benefits of an assignment here at the hardship post, China." He proceeded to tell me, "Membership in the club for us poor, deprived expatriates is US $10 per month. All of the facilities are available, except the purchase of packaged liquors to take home. But even then," he whispered, "knowing the right waiter, or bartender, can be very helpful in buying a couple of undercover bottles of wine for a party when you need it, and US $1.80 isn't bad for a bottle of Lancer's Rose, is it?"

As the drinks were served and the appropriate "welcome toasts" were offered, I glanced at my watch and remarked, "Holy smokes, it's now 8:30 in the evening! For a simple, Midwestern boy who is used to supper at 6:00 p.m., that's bedtime! Not only my watch, but my empty stomach and after four drinks, my faint head, tell me it's time I had something to eat." That was just the right cue for Penny to say, "Come with me, Sodbuster, and let's see what's cooking on the barbecue grill." As we approached the buffet-like table setup, she began, "This is really a true do-it-yourself meal." As she handed me a deep dish bowl, she explained, "At this end are the meats, beef, pork, lamb, chicken, and venison, all sliced paper thin. Take some of each or all. Fill the bottom 1/3 of your dish and then let's help ourselves to the vegetables. Again, it's pick and choose from shredded cabbage, green peppers, three kinds of onion, bean sprouts, carrots, sliced tomatoes, diced pineapple." "Now," she said, "we come to the sauces and spices where they separate the cooks and the chefs *from the boys*. Season to your taste." So, I proceeded for a total exposure experience, putting on the white wine, the soy sauce, and sugar water and took the devil-may-care approach to the sesame oil, shrimp oil, hot peppers, and coriander, and garnished the top with parsley. I had a difficult time keeping everything in the bowl and as I remarked, "My bowl runneth over," which it actually did, I'd put too much juice on.

Penny, obviously a veteran of many barbecue sessions, beckoned with a tilt of the head and a wink of the eye and said, "Come with me." Ready to set my bowl down if she did, and follow her anywhere . . . disappointed when she didn't. I followed her outdoors to a canopied area adjacent to the pool where two cooks were attending, each to a huge barbecue grill which had a roaring fire going with the flames licking out around the edges. Each of us gave our bowl to a cook, who preceded, much to my amazement, to dump all of the ingredients onto the grill and then break an egg in the middle of the ingredients. "He ruined all of my handiwork," I said as he proceeded to spread it all out on the grill with a giant-sized pair of chopsticks and then continued to push it around. I watched, fascinated, for a couple of minutes. Then Penny nudged me saying, "Now comes the coup d'é tat." At that moment, the cook swept everything off the grill right back into the bowl and didn't spill so much as a single bean sprout. Knowing that my usual hill jack phraseology, "Bulls—, or I don't believe it," wouldn't be appropriate in mixed company, I relied upon my Ivy League training and said, "Fantastic," and followed Penny back into the dining area where we picked up a pair of chopsticks and a small roll covered with sesame seeds, and then returned to our table.

By the time we got back, the rest were all busily engaged in finishing their appetizers of shrimp and crabmeat cocktails and the first entrée was being served to Ron. I noticed that the steaks and lobsters they had ordered sure looked and smelled good. But, I couldn't wait to have everyone served to begin to savor my own culinary masterpiece. As I looked at it, the thought crossed my mind and automatically popped out, "I hope this tastes better than it looks, because it doesn't begin to compare to the color and aroma of the Chinese food I had last night!"

Barry uttered a simple toast with our freshly poured Mateus Rose wine, saying "Chow," and then Penny said, "Come on, let me see how well you operate those chopsticks." I watched her as she picked up her sesame roll, squeezed it so it opened up on one end, and then began to put the barbecue mixture into the roll. Then she alternated between taking a bit of the roll and dipping in and/or taking a bit straight from the bowl. Not being an accomplished "chopstick artist," but game to try, I proceeded to play monkey-see, monkey-do. I was thinking, as I savored the first couple of bites, how can I explain this taste-experience to my family? Once again, I could only find my description to Penny to be an inadequate "Fantastic." My chopsticks crossed swords quite a bit, but before I knew it, I had made a glutton of myself and finished before everyone else. Penny, sensing my palate had been pleased, suggested, "Go ahead, eat as many bowls as you'd like." So, I did.

During my second bowl, I had to interrupt the process of feeding my face, as much as I didn't want to, to turn around to listen to a piano duo version of "Chopsticks." Barry filled me in saying, "Henry and Jimmy are the twin sons of Andy Hidalgo, the Filipino band leader. Word has it that Andy and his wife Lorna have been here at the 'O' Club since it was opened in 1951. He plays the trumpet occasionally, but he's getting in the late 50s, so he doesn't play all the time." Due to my limited vocabulary, the only word to describe their performance came out again as "Fantastic." Upon finishing my second bowl of what had to be the best of Mongolia, I debated on a third try and gave in to the encouragement of Penny who chided, "It's not fattening. Go on."

As I returned to the scene of my mealtime orgy and looked around the table to see who was there, I found myself alone. Everyone had apparently proceeded to the dance floor to enjoy the lilting, hold-me-close songs of the same sexy singer who caught my eye earlier. Almost spellbound, I liked her style and rhythm and hadn't noticed until spoken to . . . by Ron and Kathy, who had apparently been dancing and returned to the table. We immediately engaged in a conversation about the singer, and after a question and answer session of, "Who is she? Who do you think she is? I think she's the daughter of Andy. How old is she? She's no older than thirty." Answers came back like, "She's Lorna, Andy's wife. She's in her 50s, and she's the Mother of the *all* piano players." Once again, I couldn't muster up anything more descriptive than "Fantastic."

Every chance the Fraziers and the Thackers got, they danced to the slow ones and drank to the fast ones. I kind of wished my wife was here to enjoy some dancing, when Penny must have been reading my mind and she asked softly, "Do you dance to rock music?" "Not great," I replied, "but if you're game, I'd like to try," which was loud enough to be overheard and picked up by Ron who said, "Anybody heard the joke about the two Kentuckians who were coming back from a day of game hunting, empty-handed, when they met a nice country girl, stark raving nude coming down a country road. One Kentuckian tapped the other in the ribs and said, 'Watch me.' As they approached the girl, he boldly asked the fair maiden, 'Are you game?' She smiled coyly and said, 'Why? Yes,' and at that the other fellow got up and shot her." As the fellows laughed robustly and the girls blushed and made some offhand remarks, the band began to play "Big, Bad Leroy Brown . . . the Meanest Man in the Whole Damn

Town." So I asked, "Penny, you game?" To which she replied, "Sure, but don't shoot me."

After a couple of fast rock songs, the tempo slowed down and they began playing "Love Song." She came a little closer and asked, "Care to dance this one?" To which I blushingly answered, "Sure, but don't squeeze me too hard." After a couple of steps around the floor, I found myself enjoying the shape of a woman in my arms, and she tilted her head back, looked at me straight in the eyes, and testing my reaction asked, "Married?" Pushing away, I responded with subtle alarm, asking, "Why?" With that gesture, she knew the answer to her own question, which prompted the next. "How many kids do you have, and how old?" To that I again gave a tongue-tangled retort, "Why?" Flippantly, she asked, "Think I'm married?" To which I answered, "Yes." "You only get one bad guess," she said. "I'm single and Ron's sister . . . a nurse here at the American Hospital and interested in finding someone who can care." To which I reluctantly answered, to get the truth out, "I'm married . . . happily and have three teenage children and expect to bring my family to live here in two to three months." "Mind if I offer some advice?" she asked, which she proceeded to give without hesitation. "China is a man's world. If you want to be the playboy out every night like my brother who can play the game as long as he's single, don't bring your family. Assuming that's not one of life's greatest attractions for you and you plan to bring them and if you want to have one of life's greatest living experiences together, don't get caught in the foreign community social circuit. Sure, you could play bachelor every evening and take the risk of winding up with social disease and divorce or play the cocktail party and 'O' Club dinner circuit with your wife and find out your kids have become juvenile delinquents. Above all, tell the wife and the kids as much as you can that you will find it expedient occasionally to play the game of coming home a few nights with a load on or going to the girlie restaurant with the guys or to a special diplomatic function. If she and they understand the facts of life in China and if you're choosy and play the games with selectiveness, you *can* enjoy both the cake and the icing." She looked at me for what seemed to be five minutes as we continued to dance, hoping that what she had said really sank in. Then the music stopped. As we turned to go back to our table, she asked, "Do me a favor. Pack someone like yourself, only single, in your household goods when you come . . . for me."

By now, it was midnight, and Barry said, "Well, tomorrow is a work day and it's time for all good bankers to head home." He had been gracious and paid the bill without me having a chance to negotiate the damages, so as we left the dining room and I spied the one-arm bandits, I asked to buy a roll of nickels for anybody who wanted to take a chance on becoming bankrupt cheaply. Surprisingly, everybody thought that would be a great finale to the evening. Ten dollars and one hour later, I dug into my pocket and got out my last lucky coin, dropped it in the machine, and turned to walk away, when all hell broke loose, me, with a $25-RMB jackpot and no box to collect the mountain of their equivalent nickels. After cashing in, we walked out the door. I suggested to Barry that I'd prefer to walk back to the hotel, so as we parted company and said our thanks, Barry said, "Goodnight, Double Lucky . . . Lucky to be coming to China and a born gambler. Good combination."

The five-minute reverie walk back to the hotel was great. It allowed me to come to some fundamental decisions. We would not, as a family, get ourselves committed to living in a "Little America" and like the slot machines; I would play with the game, but not at it. Perhaps fate was already testing my decisions when I heard a voice as I passed a bar within a block of the hotel asking, "What room number you have at Tong Yi Da Fan Tien?" Tempted, I stopped to look at her. She was young, very attractive, nicely built, well-dressed, and very seductive. Having made my decision just minutes earlier, I said, "Sorry, Ma'am, I'm on my way to the airport to catch a flight to Hong Kong." Not to be outdone, she asked, "Take me with? We can have a good time."

Turning away, without an answer, I made it to the hotel without being further violated. Pleasant thoughts of my second day came as I quickly made my way to my room and went to bed . . . and slept . . . alone.

Chapter 6

Looking for a No. 1 Bank and Right Arm

I woke up early the next morning and lay in bed thinking aloud, "Today is my third day with only five more business days in which to accomplish 1) a visit with government officials, 2) find an office, 3) hire a secretary, 4) visit the plant site, 5) interview prospective architects, 6) shop for a car and one weekend in which to divert my interests." I knew immediately that based on the past two days that had already included two straight-out "to bed" social propositions and more business exposure than one acquires in two weeks in the United States that I couldn't afford to lay in bed. So, with a nice cool shower and a quick shave, I found myself entering the coffee shop at a few minutes before 7:00 a.m. Things were moving slowly. As I looked around, I noticed only a few of the tables occupied and a number of the employees coming in looking rather sleepy-eyed. I had to chuckle when I noticed that one of the cooks coming on duty stopped at the water fountain, cupped his hands to fill them with some water coming out of the dragon's mouth, and splashed the water on his face. I thought to myself, "Leave it to the Chinese to find some practical use for an otherwise attractive but useless piece of interior decoration."

After a very leisurely breakfast, which I thoroughly enjoyed, of a fresh fruit plate of watermelon, papaya, banana, and pineapple, I decided to head back to my room to scratch out an ad for the local English newspaper, *The China Post*, to announce my need for a secretary. As I approached the elevator, I was greeted with a "Dzao" by the female starter, which caused me to ask myself, "In how many hotels have I had the pleasure of hearing a pleasant 'good morning' or pleasant anything greeting?" The answer came back—*none*, and I concluded, "This Chinese friendliness is great."

Writing the format of the ad was easy. I only hoped the selection of a good secretary would also come with relative ease. I wondered if my usual standards for an all-American secretary ala a Chinese Jane Armstrong were too critical, but being the optimist I am, decided to shoot for the moon. So, I put the specifications down as follows:

ABC, U.S. ELECTRONICS FIRM REQUIRES EXECUTIVE SECRETARY

Capable of typing 90 WPM
With shorthand ability of 120-150 WPM
Knows accounting/cash record procedures
With mature, pleasant, and congenial personality
Not afraid of long hours and hard work
Willing to travel

Address replies to Box 100, *China Post* with resume, picture, and salary expectation and telephone number where you can be called. Interviews to be scheduled week of May 15.

I noticed that it was only 8:15 a.m., and since I didn't have an appointment at the Tenth Commercial Bank until 9:30 a.m., I decided that now would be a good time to take the ad, personally, to the *China Post*. Inquiring at the front desk, I found out from my No. 1 assistant, Patty Chen, that the office was within walking distance of the hotel. So, with her pencil map and my briefcase, I took off on foot.

Following the map, I found that it not only led me directly to the main drag, Chung Shan North Road, but past the same bars, restaurants, and nightclubs that I had passed up last night. As I approached the Butterfly Club, the scene of prior invitation, I noticed the same attraction who had wanted to know my room number and who was as cute in the daylight as she was at night. Recognizing me, she said boldly in the form of a question, "Hi, honey, you take airplane to Hong Kong?" Sheepishly, I was forced to tell a little white lie, saying, "My flight was cancelled." As I walked on, she said, almost asking, "OK, come see me tonight?" "Man," I thought to myself, "it's going to be damn tough to resist the temptation!"

Following the map, I found my way past the tourist shops, all selling the same souvenirs into a small alley, and again, flanked on both sides by small bars, restaurants, and hotels. Imagine my surprise at finding a small red and white shingle over a small entrance way establishing the location of the *China Post* next to a Hilton Hotel. Now, this Hilton was about twenty feet wide and only three stories tall, and I laughed as I looked in vain for the doorman who should be, as at every other Hilton in the world, busy opening doors on the plushest of limousines and chauffeur-driven cars. The marquee logo was the official symbol of excellence, but that was about the only degree of similarity.

But putting business before curiosity, I entered the *China Post* office and realized that one doesn't have to look for a classified ad department in this one-room office. It was obvious that all of the business functions were performed by this four-person, jack-of-all trades staff. Submitting my handwritten draft with a copy of my newly oriented business card, the young lady acknowledged her complete understanding and advised me, "I will run this ad tomorrow and Friday. OK with you?" Using a little of my newly acquired Chinese, I replied, "Ding hao," which caused a smile to come to her face, prompting a "Hsieh Hsieh Ni, Tai Le Hsien Sheng" answer.

Again, looking at my watch as I walked out onto the street, I noted that it was only 8:45 and I still had some time to kill before looking for a taxi, so curiosity getting the best of me, I decided to compare room rates at the Hilton to the $16 (Ren Min Be) (US $2) per night I was paying at the President. Entering the hotel, into a very dark cracker-box lobby, I almost felt guilty of a crime and looked back to make sure nobody was watching. I had to wake the clerk at the reception desk with a ring on their genuine bellhop bell. Awakened and startled, he jumped up and blurted out, "How long you need room?" Startled by his question, I stammered, "Why . . . for seven days I guess." To which he replied, "I rent rooms by hour, not day." I knew immediately that what I'd gotten myself into was not what I thought it would be when he asked, "Do you have girl?" Before I could even answer, he was looking around and seeing that I was alone, he slapped a key on the countertop and said, "RMB$20. You go to Room 6, and I find you a girl, kwa di, kwa di (Quickly . . . Quickly)." I knew he meant he'd have a girl here right away, so somewhat embarrassed, I turned and walked out of the door onto the street, with an obvious flushed feeling, but at the same time, quietly laughing to myself and thinking out loud, "Tai Le old-boy, you can sure get yourself exposed to the facts of life here without even trying. Now I know why they call this the greatest R&R place in the Far East. You can get propositioned and more, at any time of day, times each hour, twenty-four hours a day. Great life, *if* you don't weaken."

Making my way back to Chung Shan North Road in a hurry, I decided to catch a cab to the bank, regardless of whether or not I was going to be inappropriately, as a general manager, early for my appointment with P. C. Chiao, chairman of the Tenth Commercial Bank. I couldn't stand the prospect of any more propositions this early in the morning.

Sure as God, or Buddha here in the Far East, made little green apples, I proceeded to bump, once again, my head, knee, and briefcase as I climbed into one of the rolling wrecks . . . a Datsun Bluebird taxi. I took a statistical survey on the way downtown to try and keep my mind off the driver's maniacal tendencies on the road and accurately concluded within five minutes that nine of ten taxis had had recent wrecks, evidenced by the number tooling along with spots of body putty, primer paint exposure, and dents unrepaired. Knowing that the actual tables are damn accurate, I changed my thoughts to the day ahead and what I wanted to accomplish. My objectives were three-fold: evaluate the bank's interest, willingness, and capability to handle our local financing needs and import-export requirements; determine if the bank would be able to assist us in finding temporary office facilities in Taipei until the plant was complete; and to get all the details related to establishing my own personal banking accounts. My mental planning processes were interrupted when the driver, bringing the cab to a halt in front of an imposing Greco-Roman architectural structure, asked me the familiar question, "Hao bu hao?" With a quick glance toward the building, I looked for a sign in English. Once sighted and location of the Tenth Commercial Bank now confirmed, I answered with Hao, paid him a total of RMB$20 as indicated on the meter, and got out. I was real proud of myself when I extricated myself from the cab without banging any of my extremities.

I looked up and down the streets to get a feel of the downtown area, since this was my first venture. Perhaps because it was the downtown, the people, traffic, and business seemed to be a little more organized. Turning away with a favorable impression after my first glimpse, I entered the huge double doors of the bank and approached the counter. When I asked in English for Mr. Chiao and got a puzzled look, I repeated in unsure Chinese, "Chiao Hsien Sheng?" and offered my business card. The young girl in her school uniform blushed, whispered to another girl, and within seconds, at least a half-dozen girls were up and attending to, advising Mr. Chiao of my presence and leading me to a chair, serving me tea, and I was asking myself whether this was the height of efficiency in China or inefficiency by our standards, but the conclusion one reached was that it was a sincere desire to express hospitality.

As I sat sifting the tea leaves from the tea I was drinking, I was greeted officially by a rather conservative, mild-mannered individual who spoke perfect English and who announced himself saying, "I'm Peter Huang, manager of the bank's International Department. Welcome to the Tenth Commercial Bank of China. Would you like to follow me? We'll go right up to Mr. Chiao's office." Mr. Chiao limply shook my hand and bowed his head a little and motioned for me to have a seat next to him. Next, Mr. Chiao extended his business card in exchange for mine.

The sitting room was large but not impressive by comparison to our Western concept of the executive suite. The furniture was very ordinary, straight-backed style, and the parquet wood floor was bare of any rugs or carpet. Through Mr. Huang, I was immediately offered a choice of coffee or tea and a selection of cigarettes or cigar. The initial conversation was prompted by a series of translated questions from Mr. Chiao as to "How long have you been in China? How do you like our country? Where are you from? Do you have a family? Have you had a good Chinese meal?" The social questions and answers were certainly simple attempts to break the ice, but I was amazed to find that the whole routine, which would normally have taken less than five minutes back home, took over twenty minutes to finish in this triangle conversation with Chinese being translated to English and vice versa. Finally, the conversation was directed into the business vein. My orientation concerning the ability of the Tenth to serve ABC as a customer was almost a patterned question and answer session, which three teas and 2 hours later can be summed up to say that 1) yes, Mr. Chiao felt that the Tenth could do anything any other bank could do, 2) the Tenth would do everything within legal limits in accordance with banking regulations, 3) ABC could rest assured that their branch managers could make all the routine decisions because they were separate profit centers, and 4) the Tenth could probably find us some office space in one of the branch locations.

Mr. Chiao volunteered Mr. Huang's services to go out to look at the office space(s) available, and then asked if I were available to join him and several of his associates for dinner. When I indicated that I had prior commitments, he then asked about the next night, Thursday, to which I agreed. Mr. Chiao asked if I had been to the Mandarin Palace in the Presidential Hotel for dinner and entertainment. When I indicated that I hadn't, he asked Mr. Huang to make all the necessary arrangements. Our meeting then came to a quick end as he again shook my hand, expressed his formal interest in obtaining ABC's business, and offered a "Dzai Jen, Dzai Jen" in exchange for my translation of "good-bye."

I asked Mr. Huang, "What is the exact translation of Dzai Jen?" He explained, as we proceeded out of Mr. Chiao's office to his cubicle on the main banking floor, that, "The Chinese don't have any way to say good-bye. To say it in the English context means to part in death from loved ones, so we just say 'see you later,' which to a Chinese indicates that the hope of being together again springs eternal." I thought to myself that there was almost a touch of poetry in his interpretation, and I must always, in the future, learn to say Dzai Jen in my dealings with the Chinese people.

After a few phone calls to the branch managers to check on office space, Mr. Huang and I went out and hailed a taxi. And off we went on a tour of the city, stopping at five branches to find that none of them really fit my specifications. One was on the sixth floor of a building in a remote location without an elevator, another was much too small, a third didn't have adequate electrical facilities to hook up reverse cycle heating and cooling units, the fourth didn't have any washroom facilities, and the fifth had to be completely remodeled. Finally, we stopped a sixth time and found this time that all of the conditions were perfect. The office was located in the same building as our lawyer's office. It had plenty of space to accommodate the fifteen persons I contemplated on the pre-operations staff and was convenient to everything. It was by now 12:30, so Mr. Huang suggested, "How about going to lunch with the branch manager to talk about the rental prospects."

After a brief introduction to Mr. Shih, whose English was very broken and hesitant, we walked out of the bank around the corner, navigated our way across Nan King East Road, another major thoroughfare, dodging the bike, taxi, and three-wheel cart traffic, and then we disappeared down another of Shen Zhen's many small alleys. We stopped in front of a fenced-in house, and Mr. Huang slid back the gate to unveil an unexpected but familiar sight to me . . . a Japanese house complete with garden. Having lived in Japan a few years back as a bachelor in a "Sayonara" fashion with a Japanese girl—we were called rice-ranchers in those days—I wondered whether the description would be the same in China. As the sliding door was closed behind us, I found us observing the traditional Japanese custom of removing our shoes before stepping on the tatami-rice mat floor and watching the staff of waitresses who were all dressed in their kimono, wearing the split-toe tabi on their feet.

We were greeted by an older woman in kimono and obi, who gave us a multilingual welcome in Japanese, Chinese, and English, saying, "Hai, dozo, erashi . . . huan ying" . . . and slurring the "l's" with her "we(r)come to the Lo Ku Jo (l)estau(l)ant." She escorted us to our own private room, screened off from the rest of the outside world by the shoji-rice paper-covered doors, and we sat down at our table, on the soft tatami floors with our legs crossed.

In answer to Mr. Huang's question, "How do you like this atmosphere?" I answered "E dess!" His eyes lit up at my Japanese reply of "it's very good" and that led into a story-swapping contest about life in Japan. He advised me that he, too, had spent about one year in Tokyo, working in a Japanese bank during the day and living as a bachelor at night. Mr. Shih, explained with translation, "I, too, as a native Taiwanese have much in common with the Japanese, since the Japanese occupied the island for fifty years before the end of World War II." He amplified the ties by saying, "Most people native to the Taiwan speak Japanese and are accustomed to their habits and lifestyle." So we found ourselves very compatible as we socialized, drank our warm "Sake" rice wine, and ate "sashimi" raw fish and shrimp tempura. Frequently, I found my thoughts drifting back to my little grass shack in Hayama, remembering the pleasures of living, eating, and sleeping there. The reverie was both bitter and sweet. When the social conversation ended, which I was finding out took some time, and we got around to a discussion of business, I found Mr. Shih to be very rigid in his conditions. The rent was a reasonable US $200 per month, but he wanted ABC to make a US $50,000 deposit in his branch in a non-interest bearing account. No amount of negotiating would change his conditions, so I diplomatically changed the subject and advised Peter that it was approaching 2:00 and that I had another appointment to keep at the Tai Fong Bank and that I would advise Mr. Shih of my decision by Monday, the 6th.

Peter and I caught a cab, and he directed the driver to make haste to his competitor's bank. As we weaved in and out of traffic and played Chinese roulette at a couple of traffic circles, Peter mentioned, with noted reservations, that he would review the impasse with the chairman, Mr. Chiao, to see if he could influence a more reasonable offer for the office space, and as he let me off, he asked, "Will I see you at 7:00 p.m. tomorrow in the lobby of the Mandarin Palace?" I nodded "yes," and the taxi pulled away.

Entering the Tai Fong Bank, one would almost think you were in a carbon copy of the Tenth Commercial's main office, and I received the same reaction from the clerks when I asked for Mr. Chiang, the president. I had no more than sat down and was disappointed when I didn't get a chance to practice the art of sipping tea and sifting leaves when I spotted a very neat, well-dressed young man with a big smile coming my way in a hurry. With a very obvious glow about him, he introduced himself as C.C. Chiu, assistant manager.

As we proceeded to walk, he took an obvious interest in establishing a personal rapport in me and ABC. He inquired, "How is your treasurer, Mr. Bird?" To which I answered, "He's fine," with apprehension, obviously not aware of the extent of any prior acquaintance. As we entered the executive sitting room, he explained, as we sat and waited for Mr. Chiang, "Mr. Bird, I met once while I was at the First National Bank of Chicago on a training assignment about five years ago." As soon as Mr. Chiang finished his telephone call, we were invited into his office, which also would have passed for a carbon copy of the last bank president's office I was in. Chairman Chiang, who didn't or chose not to speak English, acknowledged our introduction by C.C., with a robust, two-handed arm shake, the right hand in a regular grip and with his left grabbed my right elbow. I was surprised by the action but knew immediately that it was his way of expressing a particularly warm Chinese welcome.

Mr. Chiang, although obviously in his 60s, was a vigorous man, and he didn't fool around in our conversation, although the conversation again took a triangular path, with C.C. doing the translation. Mr. Chiang commented, "I know of ABC well. You had a very excellent year in 1970, with record sales and earnings," even before I was able to present him with a copy of our latest annual report. With a great degree of confidence and directness, we covered my exploratory questions and their answers within forty-five minutes. As we concluded our session, he directed C.C. to make time within the balance of the afternoon to help me look for office space and then asked, "Mr. Tai Le, can you make an evening available for dinner and relaxation in Peitou with me?" Although I didn't understand Chinese, I did decipher the sound of Peitou and knew before C.C. asked that my orientation was now in high gear. I nodded my concurrence, as we shook hands and parted. C.C. didn't even bother to make telephone calls to arrange appointments. As he hustled us into a cab, he explained, "I anticipated that your company would need such facilities in your pre-formation stage, so I made prior contacts for us to look at four branch bank locations and two others offered by private parties. I have all the particulars as to size and cost, so we can sort out the fly specks from the pepper." That last comment nearly cracked me up, because it is purely a Midwest colloquialism, but it sure was the right approach, and I immediately took three proposed stops out of our itinerary. The balance of three, we canvassed in quick order, and by 4:00 p.m., we were back on our way to take a second look at the third floor office over the Tai Fong branch on Shanghai South Road, a downtown location within four blocks of their main office and ironically, across the street from their competition, the Tenth Commercial. This time C.C. took the time to introduce me to the branch manager, Mr. Wu, who spoke no English. Mr. Wu took us on a personally guided tour of the entire building. He appeared to be a tough personality, as he explained to C.C., "You will have to bear the costs of any remodeling to be done only with my OK, and pay for all utilities, maintenance, and cleaning services." As we finished the tour, we sat down at his desk which was right out on the banking floor where he could be the "king watching over the counting house" and he proceeded to lay down the terms. "Also," C.C. repeated, "ABC will have to agree to establish and maintain all of its checking and savings accounts with the branch." With his narrow feeling for our need of banking flexibility, I commented to C.C., "Based on the terms established so far, I'm beginning to reach the conclusion that Mr. Wu doesn't want to share his office space." C.C. had a few words with Mr. Wu, in Chinese, and then turned to me with a broad grin and said, "With Chairman Chiang's permission, and your acceptance of the stated conditions, Mr. Wu is prepared to let you use the space until you achieve a level of profitability rent-free." Those last two words shattered all the negotiating strategy that was building up inside me and virtually cinched my decision. But, not wanting to appear over-eager, I stated my position cautiously, "I appreciate your very generous offer, most sincerely, but I must weigh all my alternatives relative to the total objectives which I seek in establishing our banking relationships, with the many fine local and foreign-invested banking interests. I'll be prepared to give you my official answer as to our selection by Monday, the 6th." Both Mr. Wu and C.C. accepted my vague answer with a smile, and then we shook hands. C.C., translating for Mr. Wu, said, "There is one last fringe benefit that Mr. Wu would like to mention." As C.C. finished, Mr. Wu beckoned for me to follow him out of the bank through the back entrance. We exited the bank premises by walking out into a beautiful little garden area and then into the side alley. Again, C.C. translated, as Mr. Wu pointed out a small two-story wooden building ahead of us and a neat, little bar-cafe to the right of us, saying, "If you accept our offer, you will receive the fringe benefits of a lifetime membership in our neighborhood jyou-jya, a quiet little wine house, and our Flower Club, the Chinese version of your Playboy Club. Both are available after working hours for the important purpose of relaxing the business tensions." And then, Mr. Wu proceeded to step into the Flower Club to show me the intimate surroundings, and from the dimly lit interior of the inner sanctum came another of the many temptations of the Orient. About 5'5", ravishing and with an appearance of being built for comfort, Mr. Wu introduced her as Hwa Hwa, which as C.C. related, "It means Flower." My only thought was, "very appropriate for the Flower Club."

Flower did not speak very well in English, but with equipment like that, she didn't have to be a linguist. As she took my arm and gently maneuvered me to the corner settee, she softly asked, "You would like a drink, hao bu hao?" Not wanting to be put into another position of compromised moral values this early in the afternoon, I took a quick look at my watch and noted that it was almost 5:15. So, I looked at C.C. and asked for his help to retrieve myself from disaster. "C.C., can you explain to Flower that I've got an appointment at 6:30 and need to get back to the hotel, but," and stuttering a bit, "tell her I'll be back another time—you know—like Dzai Jen." Remembering that it means "hope springs eternal" too late, both C.C. and Mr. Wu laughed. Not wanting to have me embarrassed, both explained to Flower, in Chinese this time, and much to my chagrin later, that "it wasn't because I didn't want to be with her, but that there wasn't time enough for me to enjoy her . . . and we, each other to the fullest," which saved her from losing face in front of all of us.

Then, with a hasty retreat to the main street, C.C. hailed a taxi for me and told the driver, "Ching Dou, Tong Yi Da Fan Tien." As we parted, he said, "Be ready at 7:00 p.m. on Saturday. I'll pick you up. Hope you like Peitou."

As the cab pulled away, and I regained my composure, I began to review the events of the day, and without hesitation, I knew that my banking partners would be the Tai Fong Bank. To say the least, they certainly established their early reputation as being a dynamic, aggressive, decision-oriented bank with a lot of character. As the taxi pulled up in front of the hotel, I knew now that my mind was made up and my only remaining task was to outline the basis for my selection in my business reports to ABC's corporate management. Unfortunately, I knew that it would have to be without reference to the "fringe benefits package."

Chapter 7

Chinese Dinner Is Something Different and Special

Upon my return to the hotel room, I was given a note by the floor attendant, who introduced himself as Walter. I opened the note after entering the room and then loosened my tie and sat down to relax in the easy chair.

The note was from Tien Lai asking if I would like to see one of the most beautiful sights in Taiwan, suggesting Sunday, the 5th, and if so, to please call. Based on the circumstances of our first evening with the girls, I wasn't too sure as to whether the most beautiful sights would be female or truly scenery. Anyhow, my curiosity to find out caused me to make the call.

The first response on the other end, after the hotel switchboard operator dialed the number, was a feminine voice answering, "Wei, Sheng Goong Shr, Li Shiao Jai!" I didn't understand a single word, so I proceeded in English to ask, "Is Mr. Tien Lai Sheng in?" The answer, as clear in English, was, "Oh, good afternoon, Mr. Tai Le. Mr. Sheng is busy with another call right now, but he'll be with you in a couple of minutes. I'm Miss Li, Mr. Sheng's personal secretary. May I help you?" In response to my indication of Tien Lai's note about seeing the most beautiful sight in Taiwan, she continued to explain, "Oh, Mr. Sheng would like to know if you are available on Sunday to go with him to see Taroko Gorge, our beautiful marble canyon. He's asked me to arrange a tentative schedule to leave at 9:00 a.m. by FAT airlines and return by 5:30 in the afternoon and then have dinner with him at the Blue Skies later in the evening." She had already helped me make up my mind when Tien Lai came on the phone and kiddingly said, "Tai Le Hsien Sheng, I will please like to ask for your agreement not to become too familiar with Miss Li. I cannot afford to lose her to the charms of a Mei Kwo Ren, a handsome American like you." She giggled and placed her receiver on the hook for us to continue the conversation. "Tien Lai, her voice sure sounds nice and she impresses me as being very efficient. Is she nice looking?" Continuing to expose me to the language, he answered, "Ta Shing Ye hau Me Su, yeh hen pia liang." Translated that means "She is a first-class secretary and very beautiful. Further she's not available, as a secretary or otherwise . . . She's married." His last statement prompted an obvious question, "If she's Miss Li, how can she be married?" Tien Lai, laughingly, explained, "In China, it is expected that the married woman will use her family name in public to show that she is proud of her family and perhaps to demonstrate that she is, as your American women would say, 'liberated'." Changing the subject, Tien Lai asked, "Can you join me on Sunday?" "Certainly," I answered, "but let me ask one pertinent question about the transportation. Miss Li mentioned that we would fly FAT. Does that mean we're supposed to take a box lunch or plenty of money or . . ." Tien Lai, patiently answered my off-hand comments, saying, "FAT stands for Far-Eastern Air Transport. Our No. 2 airline company that flies domestic flights and is an excellent profitable company set up a couple of years ago by a couple of former Chinese Air Force pilots. Any more questions? . . . Can I arrange to get the tickets?" To which I replied, "Tien Lai, the plan sounds Ding hao." "OK," he said, "I'll meet you at the airport at 8:30 a.m. on Sunday," and with a Dzai Jen and again Dzai Jen, we hung up.

Looking at my watch, I noted that since it was now 6:30, I am going to have to hustle to be in the lobby by 7:00 to meet my sage legal counsel, T. C. Chao and son Henry. So with haste, I showered, shaved, changed suits, and was on my way to the elevator by 6:55 p.m. Upon entering the elevator, Walter acknowledged my departure by saying, "Hope you find her. Third night is a charm!" which rather struck my funny bone at the moment, but I didn't give any more thought to it as I proceeded to the lobby to keep an eye out for the Chaos. The traffic of people going out and coming into the hotel was brisk, and I enjoyed the few minutes of China-watching, mentally attempting to characterize the people as to their station in life, as a doctor, lawyer, and/or Indian Chief, chairman of the board, the buyers, the tourists, the salesmen or the Government officials. Again, I noted a predominance of young, attractive, well-dressed women in the company of elder-looking, well-off men. Before I could reach any conclusions, my thoughts were brought back to reality, as Henry Chao spotted me and called, "Tai Le, our car is out in front. Are you ready?"

The door man helped Henry and me into his chauffeur-driven 1969 Buick Electra. This time I had no problem with having to shoehorn my entrance into the car. T.C. acknowledged my presence, saying, "Good evening, Tai Le," and then gave the driver instructions, which he translated for me. "We're on our way to the Grand Hotel. Have you heard of it?" I responded to his question saying, "I have heard a great deal about the hotel and understand that it is most beautifully decorated in the classical Chinese style of architecture, but I haven't had the pleasure of seeing it, and I appreciate your interest in doing the honors." It was just a short five-minute ride up the Chung Shan North Road past the 'O' and American clubs, and as we crossed the bridge to go up the mountain, the splendor of the building came into view. "There it is!" exclaimed Henry. "And, Tai Le, for your reference, it is known as the Yuan Shan Fan Tien. You'll also hear the term, but a different character, used frequently to identify our executive, legislative, and judicial branches of government. 'Shan' means 'mountain' and 'fan tien' translates as 'dining room.' So, let's piece all this together and say the Grand Hotel is 'The restaurant on Round Mountain,' but it also has hotel room accommodations."

As we got closer to the building, the grandeur and the beauty of the structure in its regal, mountain-top setting became more apparent. When we drove up the winding road, I marveled at the artistic craftsmanship of the gardeners, who must have spent hundreds of hours in the landscaping and sculpturing the bushes into the shapes of animals. Every rock, stone, and flower looked like it had been placed into this jigsaw puzzle of manmade beauty, piece by piece. We pulled up to the front entrance under an extended canopy, and as we got out, I asked, "T.C, Henry, would you mind if I took a few minutes to walk around on the outside, while it's still light?" T.C. answered, "Henry, you go with Tai Le and give him the background, while I go arrange for our table." With just one question from me as the stimulus, Henry proceeded to relate, "The main building you see here was opened in 1948, as a government guest house, and was used for hosting and lodging of foreign diplomatic parties. A government corporation was established under the direction of Madame Chiang Kai Shek, and several additional sections were added, like the Jade and Phoenix Halls you see here, and it was opened to the public as a hotel. On the drawing board is a new addition planned to be ready for occupancy soon, and it will be a twelve-story building done in the same classic Chinese architectural style and will double the capacity. You know, China is really emphasizing the tourist trade. Not only does it bring in valuable foreign exchange, but as important, it opens us up to the eyes of the world in this period of political conflict with the mainland. We hope people will like what they see and remember us favorably." Having almost done a circle tour of the building, Henry asked, "Shall we go back to the main pavilion and join my father?" As we approached the main building, I had to stand back and take a long look. "It certainly is a beautiful and graceful building. You know, Henry, one can't really appreciate all the compliments that others lavish on this art treasure, unless you see it with your own eyes. It's hard for the Westerner to imagine that this kind of art, architecture, and craftsmanship still exists in our modern-day 'go-go' world." The intricacy of the building with its glazed roof and cornice figurines and its gentle unswept eves, the interlocking jigsaw puzzle-like roof structure, and the exquisite richness of the gold leafing and the red lacquer from the roof down to the ground line could really be studied and enjoyed for hours." Henry broke my image of old China through the "looking glass," gently suggesting, "Shall we take a look on the inside?" As we walked into the spacious lobby through two giant double doors opened by door attendants, who were dressed and looked like Johnny—the Philip Morris boy of years past, he began again to explain, "The interior decor with the central, white, marble staircase guarded by the temple lions and the ground-level side anterooms is a duplicate of the layout of the Imperial Palace in Beijing." We stood at the base of the stairs a few minutes, as he continued, "In the old days, a guest or courier could only see the Emperor and Empress by going through a long, lengthy process of interview by the official staff and only after being cleansed of mind and body by attendants-in-waiting. All of this process took place by progressing through a series of anteroom interviews such as these, until all the tests of faith and loyalty had been performed and the person given permission to enter the Imperial Sanctuary by climbing these heavenly steps for an audience." Now, as we began to climb the steps, I felt almost as if I had been exposed to the ritual. As we walked slowly and softly up the stairs, one could almost feel relieved of the burdens of the outside world. At the top of the first landing hung a beautiful and ethereal Chinese-scroll silk painting. At the top of the second flight, we came into a large open room. The ceiling was done in wood-lacquered panels, each resplendent in their rich combination of gold, blue, and red colors. Henry said, "Each of the panels present the Chinese character for 'luck' and are complemented by the dragon and phoenix bird who by Chinese legend were love partners. This room is used as a setting room, but frequently is opened up for receptions." The furniture was all done Chinese-style covered rich, ornamental upholstery, arranged in sets of four units, two chairs, and two divans around a centerpiece oriental rug, obviously handwoven. The walls were tastefully decorated with a variety of wood carvings, scroll paintings, and offset by intricately carved wooden screens. After lingering for a moment to absorb the splendor, we turned to walk toward the dining room. We spotted T.C, already seated at the table near the window with a beautiful view out over a river basin, plains area with a glimpse of another ominous Chinese-style shrine gate. T.C. began the conversation by saying, "Huan Ying . . . Welcome, Tai Le Hsien Sheng. Hen hao fun jing, a? "Isn't this a beautiful and tranquil view?" "Words are not adequate to describe the positive feeling that one receives from this experience," I answered.

T.C. asked if I would like something to drink before we ate, suggesting, "That will give us a chance to go over the menu and select some dishes that you would enjoy. The hotel offers both a Cantonese and Szechuanese style of cuisine, with a few Beijing specializations. The Cantonese being a sweet and sour sauce type of cooking and the Szechuan is very hot and spicy." T.C. asked, "Have you tasted the Chinese rice-wine Hsiao Shing, or would you prefer to stick to the Western drinks, beer or scotch?" Not wanting to offend my hosts and secretly wanting the opportunity to try everything to establish my taste bud preferences, I opted for both, saying, "If you have no objections, T.C, I'll start with a scotch and water and then switch during the meal to the drink of your choice." So, he ordered, in Chinese, a selection of each.

In response to T.C's and Henry's interrogation as to what dishes I might like, we agreed to a selection of several dishes from each menu, the description of which sounded like a real venture into a gourmet's delight. T.C. ordered, in Chinese, and then translated for my benefit, saying, "To start, I asked for a peacock cold cuts dish with thousand year eggs. Then to follow, some minced squab—Beijing style, spiced honeyed ham, shark fin soup, an order of fried shrimp balls, Szechuan chicken, sweet and sour yellow mandarin fish, frogs' legs in pepper and spices, turtle soup, mushrooms, bamboo shoots and green vegetables, Beijing duck—three way—will be the last course." I commented, "T.C, do you have other guests coming for dinner? You've ordered enough for an army." T.C. and Henry smiled, and Henry said, "Tai Le, eat some from each dish, not a lot, but you must sample our best dishes."

The drinks were served and T.C. offered an immediate toast to my scotch and water and his gin and tonic, "May our friendship and our business relationship, both be infinitely successful. Sui bien (which means 'as you like it'), Tai Le." We drank without being hurried as in most Western restaurants. Soon the beautiful shrine with its ominous gate again captured my interest, so I asked, "What's that beautiful structure over there?" T.C. answered very softly, "That's our martyr's Shrine . . . Where we pay homage to those persons, military men, and civilians who have given their lives in defense of our government in our struggle for freedom." Almost as if by plan, the lull in the conversation was broken by the serving of our first dish, the peacock and thousand year eggs. "It almost look too beautiful to eat," I commented. Responding, Henry explained, "Remember my mention of the Phoenix? It is one and the same as your definition of the Peacock. The Phoenix is a symbol of 'love' to Chinese, and the Thousand Year Eggs symbolic of the hope of longevity among our people. The eggs, after being dyed in tea, will help to promote one's long life." As Henry explained, T.C. began to take small pieces from the plate and to serve me. When everybody had a selection of the small pieces of chicken, turkey, pork, tongue, abalone, and the carved radish flowers, T.C. offered a new toast, this time with the traditional rice wine, Shiao Hsing, saying, "Gam bei (which means the same as 'bottoms up')," and down the hatch it went. T.C. and Henry grimacing to the taste, then showed me their empty glasses, about the size of a shot glass, until I too had emptied mine and could show. I realized that this was their way of showing drinking courage and avoiding the embarrassment of "losing face," which is extremely important to the Chinese, as I began to recognize more perceptively from their actions and words.

Each succeeding dish became a new experience in tantalizing the taste buds. Not only did each taste superb, but each of the dishes were exquisitely decorated in their preparation and smelled 'fantastic.' T.C. offered a beer or rice wine toast before every new course, and through this evening of gastronomic pleasure, the theory behind Chinese cooking came out. A true Chinese dish must meet three basic requirements: first, it must look appetizing and the cook will appeal to your sense of color by decorating the dish; second, the food must have a pleasing aroma tempting you to try; and third, it must succeed in appealing to and satisfying your tastes. Not only must the chef be an artist, but the host must carefully plan the menu, as his guests will judge his selections and the order in which they are served as an indication of his awareness of the rules of etiquette and social class. Ten to twelve courses are normal to expect . . . the more the better in terms of displaying your wealth. A good host should plan to serve more food than can be eaten and hopes to have much left over. The guest should respond by taking some of each dish, and it is considered polite to burp or belch out loud. A person's enjoyment of the meal will be judged by looking at the area around his dish. If food particles, spots, and stains are evident on the table cloth, that's a sign you thoroughly enjoyed the meal. I kept thinking to myself that each succeeding dish was better than the previous one. I wasn't able to limit my sampling to one helping of each dish and was getting uncomfortably full, but I wasn't about to give up, or cause my hosts to "lose face" thinking I didn't enjoy the meal. The beer and or rice wine before each course also had a definite mellowing effect.

The more we drank, the more topics of conversation we opened for discussion of our thoughts, and I was pleased that we were able to feel at ease in discussing such delicate issues as the United Nations, the war in Vietnam, the problems of world economy, and Nixon's visit to China very introspective. We also covered a number of less crucial areas like sports interests and family. About the time that we were being served the last remnants of our Beijing duck, a delicious soup broth made from the carcass right before our eyes, I broke the train of conversation with a very loud and noticeable belch which caused me to blush in embarrassment, causing others around us to stare at my hosts to laugh. T.C. exclaimed, "Tai Le Hsien Sheng, you'll make a perfect fit into our culture . . . and be totally accepted into society. Now, let's have some fresh fruit and tea for our last course."

As we sipped our tea, T.C. leaned forward and asked, "Tai Le Hsien Sheng, what do you think of our country so far?"

Answering diplomatically, I said, "T.C, to be very honest, I have been favorably impressed in these first few days. Frankly, I have observed many positive signs. I'm sure that there are some negative ones, but so far I haven't experienced any." His face lit up, with obvious pleasure, and he said philosophically, "I'm pleased that you are positive, but disappointed that you have not been exposed to the negative so, I would like to continue our orientation with a living lesson in exposing our age-old theory of 'Yin and Yang,' the Confucian belief that there are two opposite forces which attract, and they ultimately result in achieving a state of equilibrium in our lives."

CHAPTER 8

The Lighter Side of Chinese Life

As we walked out of the hallowed halls of the Grand Hotel, T.C. held onto my arm and talked to me like a father, calling me by my first name, saying, "Tai Le, it is important that you understand the Yin and Yang theory because it is the main thread of our culture. The words Yin and Yang have many meanings, but for one 'Yin' definition, there is always an opposite 'Yang' meaning. For example, Yin can be interpreted to mean female. Yang, likewise, carries the meaning of male." So engrossed was he in wanting to make his explanation clear to me, we sat down in the lobby and he pulled out a piece of paper and listed the many word definitions of both and handed the paper to me. The definitions for Yin were listed on the left and Yang on the right.

<u>Yin</u>	<u>Yang</u>
Female	Male
Negative	Positive
Moon	Sun
Earth	Heaven
Cloudy	Clear

T.C. continued, "Tai Le, I want you to understand that all the 'Yin' characters are negative. This does not mean they are bad. It takes forces from both directions to achieve the desired balance so important to our lives as we relate to politics, economics, our weather, and our relationship to others. Am I making myself clear?" Thinking to myself that the concept was so simple, I wondered how come it hadn't been expressed by our Western ancestors in such a clear picture, and I acknowledged, "T.C, it is very clear and logical, and I accept the theory completely."

"Good!" he exclaimed, as he stood up and said, "Now, let's expose you to some of our good negative forces." As we get into the car, Henry gave the driver instructions to go to CIRO's, after which he and his father proceeded to give me an explanation. "Tai Le, my father and I would like to take you to CIRO's, a well-known dance hall." T.C. then chimed in, "The good negative element in this experience is that Yin and Yang get together to dance. Again, two opposites attract to each other, for the purpose of mutual interest. The man to enjoy himself, relaxing in the company of a young attractive woman, and the woman, while pleasing the man, creates an opportunity to earn a comfortable living." Henry interjected with an explanation of the rules. "When we get there, you will have a selection of girls to choose from, or Father and I can arrange, with the manager, for a girl who speaks English for you to dance with. The girl will stay with you for three dances, and then, if you do not want her and would like to look for another partner, she is free to rotate to other tables." T.C. then counseled, saying, "If you find a girl you would like to keep as your dance partner for the evening, let me know and I'll arrange it with the manager. If you would like to take her home, later in the evening, then you will have to negotiate the arrangement on your own. If you should need translation services, Henry or I will be available on a no-fee basis, until you return to your hotel room." With a chuckle to his voice, he said, "By then, you shouldn't need any further assistance. Hao bu hao?"

Arriving at the entrance, with its glittering marquee, one might have assumed that we had arrived at CIRO's in Las Vegas. The doorman promptly opened the car doors, and we walked into the building receiving first-class, red carpet treatment. The atmosphere was one of plushness with the red pile carpet, red velvet wall covering, and a real authentic cut-glass sparkling chandelier. A maître d' in his resplendent tuxedo took our names and checked the table reservation. Henry told him, in Chinese, that we would like to review the available ladies, so he escorted us to a very plush sitting area where at least fifty very lovely females were seated. A quick glance around revealed possibly fifty tables around the dance floor. Listening to the dance band play the latest popular music, I guessed at least fifty couples to be dancing and as many conversing, drinking tea, and holding hands at their tables. T.C. interrupted my observations, asking, "See any girls you'd like to share the evening with? Do you want someone who speaks English?" Answering with some reservation, I said, "T.C, I'll trust my luck to your judgment and taste." Obviously pleased at my expression of confidence, he placed my order with the maître d', and then I followed as we exited the first floor main hall and took an escalator up to the second floor where we entered a much smaller, more exclusive, intimate, and obviously higher class dance floor room where we were seated. Although the band was much smaller, playing to this intimate group of fifteen tables, the music was quieter and designed to set a more romantic atmosphere. Henry explained that our girls should be here in a few minutes, and further, "If you want to get away from the music and be alone with your girl, there are anterooms available where one can indulge in the comfort of a sitting room to drink and talk *and* . . ." He didn't continue his sentence, leaving the final words to one's imagination.

The maître d' brought out three companions, whom T.C. introduced. It was obvious that he knew all of them. Their names matched their beauty. Shwei Fong, the oldest and most mature looking, was T.C's favorite. She sat down quietly and didn't take her eyes off T.C. as she began to stroke the back of his neck. Henry's very alive and alluring partner, Li Li, immediately began a conversation in Chinese with him, and within thirty seconds, they were headed for the dance floor. T.C. introduced me to a very sweet, rather quiet, and somewhat bashful Lin Fong, who, despite her timid manner, began our conversation by apologizing, "Tai Le Hsien Sheng, I not speak English very well, but I try to make you enjoy this night." Her apology rather humbled me into answering, "Hsieh Hsieh Ni," which she immediately took as a compliment, saying, "Ah, you speak very good Chinese. You know our language?" Again, I struggled to answer in Chinese, wanting her to know I had learned a few phrases, so I said, "Wa showa yi den dien (meaning I speak very little)." The chemistry between us was confirmed, through her slow, brown eyes, as she remarked, "Hen hao le."

We sat and talked softly, trying to learn more about each other. I expected her to react unfavorably when I told her that I was married and had three children, two in their early teens. Instead, she seemed more interested, asking, "May I see their pictures?" She commented, as I showed her a family picture, "Ni de Tai Tai, hen mai ling," which she translated, saying, "Your wife . . . She is beautiful!" I caught myself thinking that this situation was a paradox . . . surely, if a similar companion scenario was played in the States, the last thing the broad would want to know would be if you have a wife and, if the fact came out, then she'd likely give you an immediate cold shoulder. Ling Fong, who didn't look older than a sweet sixteen or seventeen, was actually twenty-one, the eighth child in a family of eleven, a college graduate in Chinese literature and working to support three younger brothers and sisters in high school and university. I asked during the course of our conversation where she lived, to find to my amazement that not only did she live at home, but her parents knew of her work. My typical Occidental reaction was to ask, "Lin Fong, are you telling me the truth?" Hurt, she said, "You ask Chao Hsien Sheng." Her story, previously confirmed by T.C, now put me back on the pursuit. Her honesty was rather enlightening, despite the shadow of her occupation.

After talking for perhaps forty-five minutes, she reached for my hand and asked, very shyly, "Tai le Hsien Sheng, would you like to dance with me?" Despite my apologies that I didn't dance well, she led me to the dance floor and snuggled herself softly in my arms and initiated the first steps as if she was subtly leading. The music was very soft and romantic, and as much as I wanted to resist her charms, I couldn't help the feeling coming over me.

It came to mind that I hadn't had this schoolboy feeling since before I was married and that it had probably been two years since I had last danced with my wife, Although I was developing a guilt complex, I was enjoying the experience. Lin Fong was no more than five feet and, although nicely built, was probably not more than ninety pounds. She almost seemed to be a feather in my arms, and her soft curves seemed to fit very close and nicely. After quietly dancing for almost fifteen minutes without a word spoken, she looked up at me and asked, "You enjoy dancing with me?" To which I answered honestly, "Very much, Lin Fong." We danced on for a long while without further talk, and I was oblivious to time. Finally, Lin Fong asked, "Tai Le Hsien Sheng, should we not go back to take tea?" Nodding yes, she led me into one of the small side rooms where we sat down on a sofa. The first thing she asked as she poured the tea into two tall glasses was, "Are you happy with me tonight?" My very guarded answer was, "Yes, why?" She answered with another question, "Do you want to take me back to your hotel?" Flattered but disappointed, knowing that no matter how much I'd like to, that I didn't want to take a guilty conscience home to my wife, and being more practical, possibly a case of something more serious, I decided to set the record straight as to my intentions. So, probably sounding like a father, I said, "Lin Fong, you have flattered me into thinking that I am attractive and desirable, but my rational mind says that you aren't propositioning me because of a real feeling of love, but for the money involved. Now, I'm a married man with two teenagers. I'm almost old enough to be your father. I don't have any intention of taking advantage of you. If . . . if your physical attraction tonight was for real, I wouldn't want to buy your love." Pausing for effect, I continued, "Why did you ask me? Do you really want to go to bed with me? How about the men that you dance with tomorrow and the day after?" Before I could finish, I could tell that I had made my point. Her head was tilted down, her face was red, and she looked tearfully at me and said, "Tai le Hsien Sheng, my boss says I must make men happy. I must ask them if they want to take me home . . . If I don't, I will lose my job and I must work to support my family. I want to have a real honest job, but as a teacher, I cannot make enough. Please forgive me for making you angry. I want you to love me, not for sex, but as a person."

With that statement, I said, "Lin Fong, let's go. I want to take you out of here." She accepted meekly, and we went back to the table to sit down with T.C. and Henry. "T.C," I said, "how do I arrange to take Lin Fong home with me?" Pleased that his choice of women was right for me, he motioned for the maître d' and, after signing a chit, he spoke to Lin Fong in Chinese, and she took my hand to lead me home. I said my farewell to T.C. and Henry in a hurry, promising, "I'll call you tomorrow."

As we left CIRO's and got into another one of those knee-busting Bluebird taxis, she instructed the driver, in Chinese, a little of which I could understand. "Hsien Sheng, Tong Yi Da Fan Tien, kwa di kwa di." As we sped back to the hotel, I asked, "Lin Fong, how much did Chao Shien Sheng pay for your release?" "RMB$250," she answered. Doing some mental arithmetic, that came out to US$31. I asked, "How much of that do you get?" She replied "RMB$50." Again, my arithmetic calculations revealed that if she went home accompanied on twenty evenings each month, her total income would be only US $125 per month plus any gratuities she might receive. I asked, "Could I buy your permanent release from your job?" Her face reddened, and she said, "Tai Le Hsien Sheng, that would be very expensive . . . maybe RMB$12,500." "Can't you just quit?" I asked. "Yes, only if I can pay. But I could never find a job to pay my debt and support my family. Tai Le Hsien Sheng, I could not expect and would not accept my release, even if you thought to pay. That would not be fair. In three years, my brothers and sisters will finish school, and by then, I will have earned enough for my lao ban (Boss) that he will let me go. Then, I will find a respectable job and then I hope to find a man who will hide my past in our love for each other, forever."

As we arrived at the door to the President Hotel, I paid the driver and Lin Fong proceeded to get out after me. Gently, I closed the door saying, "No, Lin Fong, as much as I would like to take you to my room, it would not be right. I will give the driver money to take you home." After giving the driver RMB$40 for fare, I tried to give her RMB$125, thinking it would perhaps in some small way compensate her for the indignities she must suffer. She refused, thrusting the money back into my hand, saying, "No, Tai Le Hsien Sheng, I do not want to be bought. I want you to think well of me. Will you promise to come back to see me again? Hao bu hao?" I couldn't refuse the invitation, so I acknowledged as humbly as I could, in Chinese, with a simple "Hao," and with a wink to seal the bargain, she ordered the driver to drive on.

As I got my key and walked to the elevator, I couldn't help but think deeply about the great differences in the Oriental's acceptance of indentured service versus our Occidental Laisse Faire business concept in this age-old trade. In many respects, the obligation is much more final, but also I marveled at the spirit in which it is practiced and accepted . . . almost within a feeling of tenderness . . . quite different than the crude, hard, cold, flesh peddling atmosphere typical of the Occidental purveyors.

Just as the elevator doors began to close, an elderly Chinese gentleman and his pretty little companion joined me. When I smiled, they both acknowledged, returning the communication with a smile. I knew that my prior thoughts of fathers and their daughters had been naive, and I wondered if he, as an Oriental, had some of the same thoughts about his relationship as I, an Occidental, as to right and wrong. T.C.'s explanation of Yin and Yang was fresh in my mind as I got off the elevator, and Walter, who saw me without a companion, asked, "Tai Le Hsien Sheng, you have no luck tonight?" To which I answered, "Sorry, Walter. No luck tonight."

Chapter 9

Government from a Different Light

It felt great to wake up leisurely with no pressure to meet a schedule. It had been a long time since I enjoyed the luxury of waking at 9:00 a.m., but, since I had no morning appointments today, I hadn't set my alarm or left a call at the desk for a morning wake-up. So, I turned on some soft, wake-up music on the bedside radio console and decided that I'd read the morning newspaper and ease into a late breakfast with plenty of time to spare before my scheduled 2:00 p.m. appointment with Minister Tseng of the Ministry of Business Affairs (MOBA) to discuss the filing of our FIA (Foreign Investment Application). After a quick face wash, shave, and completion of constitutional duties, I picked up the *China Post*, which the hotel furnished each morning as a complimentary copy, sliding it under the door. A quick glance at the headlines was encouraging for China's future, as the MOBA announced an integrated steel mill project with US Steel for completion in 1975. As I flipped the paper to continue the article on the bottom-half, I noticed an ad that raised a hearty chuckle.

It read:

    ABC, U.S. Electronics Firm
    Needs Sexretary

It wasn't quite so funny when I realized that the ad was mine. My instant embarrassment was overcome by a mad dash to the phone. "Give me the *China Post*," I blurted to the hotel operator. By the time the call was placed, I could feel a slow burn coming on, and this turned immediately to severe communications frustration when a female voice on the other end answered in Chinese, and kept repeating, "Waw bu dung" (I do Not Know) to my questions as to the availability of the editor. After ten "Waw bu dungs," I gave up my attempts to communicate by phone and resolved to make a personal visit to ask for a retraction.

Within fifteen minutes, I was dressed and out the front door of the hotel doing a half-dog trot to the *China Post*, with a copy of the paper in my hand. As I got to the busy corner on Chung Shan North Road, waiting for traffic to clear so I could cross, I realized that my emotions were racing ahead of my judgments, so I decided to compose myself and walk into their office in full possession of all my faculties . . . which I did.

As I entered the door and approached the business counter, my hostilities subsided when the cute little girl behind the counter looked up, smiled, and said, "Good morning, Mr. Tai Le. How you like your ad? Front page, pretty good, yes?" Somewhat puzzled by her amusement at my misfortune, I decided to remain calm, so I acknowledged her questions with a polite, "OK . . . May I see the editor?" With a prompt "Yes, sure" and an indication that she suspected nothing was wrong, she took me through the counter gate to a very small office at the back of the room where she left me after a few words, in Chinese, to speak to Miss Wang.

Acknowledging my presence, Miss Wang said in perfect English, "Good morning, may I help you? I am the editor." I knew from her command of the language and her general presence that this attractive, middle-aged woman would have an answer and solution to what I had to say, so I decided to initiate and maintain a very mature conversation. "Can you help me keep from 'losing face' with my Western friends?" It was my lead-in statement. A broad smile came across her face when I showed her the ad on the front page, and then she said with all sincerity, "My humble apologies, Mr. Tai Le. Although I find our mistake somewhat humorous, I sympathize with your complaint. I guarantee that an appropriate retraction will be made and the ad corrected. I would like to suggest that we also run it one additional day at our expense, if this meets with your approval?" "Miss Wang," I answered, "I know that what has been done will be difficult to correct and appreciate your willingness to take that action. However, I would also appreciate your explanation of why it happened." Confidently, she said, "I will find out and let you know, and I will also talk with two very fine secretaries that I know to suggest they submit their resumes for your consideration. Is that a fair bargain?" My answer, "Nie hao" was favorably received and our future relationship sealed when she extended her hand as a gesture of agreement and friendship. "After you leave, I will talk with my employees. If I do so now, in front of you, I will cause them to lose great face and risk the danger of them leaving their jobs. I hope you understand?" I left the office, satisfied that the matter would be handled properly, but knowing that my present and future exposure to some good-natured ribbing would require some quick verbal responses.

Back in my hotel room, now too late to eat breakfast and too early to eat lunch, I decided to put together a quick report to the boys back at "hum drum" corporate headquarters. Believing that the best defense is a good offense, I decided to spice up my report with a copy of the ad. About half-way through my report, I heard a faint knock on the door. Answering it, I was surprised to find the cute little girl from the *China Post* office standing there with obvious discomfort, her head down, quietly asking, "Mr. Tai Le, I am Miss Chao. May I come in to explain?" She stood very meekly, her head bowed as I let her in. She refused to take the seat I offered her. She broke the moment of silence, saying, "I am very sorry, Mr. Tai Le, for my mistake. I meant no harm. In the American movies, we always see a beautiful girl as the secretary, so I changed the wording to make sure you got only the most beautiful Chinese girls for your job. I hope you are not angry with me?" As I said, "Shiao Jai (Madam)," she looked up, her eyes sparkling with innocence. Continuing, I spoke softly, "I cannot be angry with you. I appreciate your intentions as being honest."

Admonishing her a little, I said with firmness, "In the future, however, be careful not to take liberties with the copy unless previous approval is granted by the customer." Then to relax the tension, I extended my hand and chided, "I hope, like you, that I can find a secretary who is as beautiful as You are . . . smart and efficient." Quietly and confidently, she replied, as she backed out of the room, bowing, "Thank you, Tai Le Hsian Sheng, for your kindness. I will help you find the right one."

As I closed the door, I had no doubt that her actions were those of sincerity . . . that her apology was not prompted by her employer. It took a great deal of courage to admit her mistake, personally . . . and I was confident that I would see a candidate of her choice. After a quick wrap-up on the draft of my report, I found myself privately chuckling to a vivid imagination of what kinds of thoughts the prospects might have when reading the ad and wondering how my candidates would look. Noticing that it was now noon, and my previously intended quiet morning was now gone, I decided it was time for a quick lunch and then to be off to pick up Henry Chao on our way to visit with Minister Tseng.

I took another of those insane rides in a taxi with an Oriental "Evil Knievel" at the wheel to the Chao's law office, from where we proceeded by private car. T. C. had other business to attend to, so Henry and I mapped out our plans for the afternoon session with Minister Tseng. Henry summarized our thoughts, saying, "Remember, this being your first visit with Minister Tseng, it should be more of a courtesy call, with a brief statement of your company's objectives in wanting to make your foreign investment here in China. He'll probably have one of his deputies there, Mr. C. Liao or Lawrence Li, who he will designate to work out all the nitty-gritty details with us in future sessions." As we left the downtown area and proceeded to drive through the governmental section of the city, Henry was quick to point out the Presidential Palace, "Here is our equivalent to your White House." I looked back at it, as we turned the corner and drove down a wide street, which was obviously used for parade grounds during celebrations. It was a very impressive large red brick building surrounded by royal palm trees, and the portico balcony was adorned with a massive map of the Mainland China and the China Sea. Off the coast sure looked insignificant by comparison with the land mass of the total country. Henry redirected my attention to a traditional Chinese gate looming in front of us, saying, "This is one of the five original gates of the city. Beijing, you know, was once a walled city. Sometime during the World War II, the wall was torn down as the city expanded beyond the limits of the wall to contain it." Just then, our driver engaged us in another game of Chinese Roulette, taking us for a quick spin into and out of the traffic circle around the gate, and then shortly after, we entered a boulevard lined with royal palms. It reminded me of Miami. The setting was regal . . . except for the architecture of the buildings, which was mixed contemporary oriental and nineteenth-century European. Our car pulled up into the driveway of the MOBA . . . located in a very new, modern, and efficient-looking building.

It was only 1:40 p.m., still leaving plenty of time before our two o'clock meeting with Minister Tseng, so he offered, "How about a cook's tour before we go up?" A number of interesting exhibits had been set up in the lobby of the building to depict the economic development plans and progress of the past ten years. Henry explained, "These three dimensional models show the shorelines and the locations of the duty-free industrial ports and manufacturing zones that the country has completed and planning for the future. These port zones are designed so that a company interested only in manufacturing for export can import raw materials, process them, and then export without going through any of the complex and time-consuming customs requirements. These interior sites also provide for a dual purpose, a company that is approved to sell into our economy, yet have duty-free exemption on its manufactured goods for export can locate in an industrial park. This doesn't mean that you're required to locate in a government zone. However, if you want to locate on a private piece of land, that's possible too, as long as you're willing to fence the plant in and provide for a resident customs official, who will open, inspect, and or seal all incoming and outgoing materials which must be bonded. The customs people are constantly striving to work with our investors, like ABC, to streamline the process. Now, here is the Nei Li Industrial Park, where your land option is located." With this explanation, we then walked around looking at the product and color-picture displays on the walls depicting the representative industries along the coastlines. The sophistication of the many products clearly emphasized the advanced state of industrialization in their electronics, textile, and recreation industries. The pictures of the plants, both inside and out, reflected the latest in architectural style and manufacturing process. "This presentation is really impressive," I said, "and I see from this display over here that a fully integrated steel mill project is on the drawing boards for 1998. Great progress!"

With that we mounted the stairs to the third floor to keep our appointment on time. Henry commented wryly, "The normal rules of business protocol about being late don't apply when you're meeting with the minister, unless, perhaps, you happen to be GIMO." We entered an outer reception area, where Henry introduced me to P.C. Wu, the minister's appointment secretary. After the usual exchange of business cards, Mr. Wu extended the hospitality of his office. "Would you like to have a seat for a few minutes? Minister Tseng won't be long. Would you enjoy some tea or coffee?"

Henry and I sat down and indicated our preference of tea to the cute, little school-uniformed tea girl, and no sooner than the leaves had settled, we were ushered into the minister's office.

"Good afternoon, Tai Le Hsian Sheng. Let me say that I've been looking forward to making your acquaintance. Please have a seat." My initial reactions to the minister were very positive. He was a very good-looking man, tall for a Chinese, well dressed, and moved with a great deal of poise. The office was also impressive in comparison to those I'd been in within the business community. Besides being spacious and tastefully decorated, it had a nice view of the outside boulevard. The chairs were comfortable as well as functional. All in all, the entire setting created a positive image of the economic well-being and planning for the country's future.

Minister Tseng carried the conversation in very general terms, explaining about the country's economic planning process and achievements. "In the mid-1970s, we implemented the four-year economic plan concept. We're now on our fifth four-year plan. The results have been excellent. We've never failed to achieve our plan. In fact, I hope I'm not bragging when I tell you that we've had numerous economic groups from Asia and Africa come to learn and actually see first-hand, how we do it. We have received economic assistance from your government to help us develop our infrastructure and industrial base, but we're very proud of the fact that we haven't been dependent on the United States for aid since 1975. Since 1970, we've been able to generate a favorable balance of foreign exchange reserves. In 1971, we achieved a $4 billion plus two-way trade balance." With extreme pride, he declared, "We have, in fact, outproduced in our foreign trade account comparisons." Then, with a humbleness transcending his previous expression of confidence, the minister stated, "We have known for some time now that our future position in the world of nations lies not in our diplomatic and political friendships but in the strength of our economy in our dealings with ours. We feel we have generated many positive relationships and gained respect for our ability to compete."

"Now," he said, "changing the subject to a more personal vein, tell me a little bit about yourself and your company, ABC." His stated interest in me, as a person, and the fact he knew of our company by name impressed me, for I am sure that he meets and deals with many hundreds of people outside the government boundaries.

Not wanting to be overbearing, I proceeded to outline the background of our company. Knowing that age establishes a measure of respect, in Chinese philosophical evaluations, I began by saying, "Minister Tseng, ABC is a well-established company, having celebrated its fiftieth anniversary in 1969." I could tell that that statement immediately gave him a sense of comfort knowing that we were not a fly-by-night company. Intentionally, I continued to capitalize on this inroad to Chinese logic to emphasize, "ABC is also a very financially strong and sound business, ranking in the Fortune Top 500 Corporations in the United States in each of the last ten years in sales and in the top hundred on their shareholder stock return on investment. However, I want to emphasize that our overall bigness does not mean that we are a mechanical management. Our concept of organization is designed to promote the human relations aspects of our dealings with customer, shareholder, employees, and suppliers. We like to keep our operations decentralized, such that no one of our plants has an employment level of more than five hundred to six hundred people. Each of the plants are designed to operate as a separate unit, with their own policies and procedures suited to meet the requirements of their market, product, and geographic and governmental environments. Fundamentally, we believe that *people* are our most important resource, and we feel strongly that establishment of a 'family' feeling within the company, within each plant, is the key to our past and future success." Pausing to let the impact of those statements register and to anticipate a comment or question, I found the minister listening intently, and when he nodded his understanding as a signal to proceed, I then began to outline the basic objectives of our considering and investment in China. "We're interested in building a facility in the Far East, to add consumer product capacity worldwide, and then expand to eventually replace our production facilities in the United States. Initially, we want to export 100 percent, but would, after satisfying those market demands, like to establish a demand for our products within the local and South East Asian market sphere. Ideally, we'd like to start out producing a complete line of radios and then graduate into the more sophisticated electronic stereo equipment products. We want to maintain our family concept of a manageable employment level of six hundred people limit, with the minimum expatriate management involvement. Hopefully, the plan productivity could yield FOB values of US $25-30 million in exports, if everything we hear about the efficiency of local labor is true. However, I want to emphasize that although our product processes are 'labor intensive,' the most important reason for wanting to locate in the Far East is to be close to our supply sources of component materials. We will be dependent upon the ability of your economy and government to promote development of local suppliers of quality parts. Of course, we stand ready to help in this respect. If all goes well in our initial investment, we expect to consider further expansion of our investment interests within a period of two to three years."

At this point, I thought it best to pause again to let the minister collect his thoughts and offer a reaction. Although his interest appeared keen, he was not anxious to respond. It was obvious that he wanted me to play out my entire hand so that he could then dictate the terms of our entry. Sensing this motive, I decided to switch my tactics to provoke a response. Taking a diplomatic approach, I hoped to employ the cat-and-mouse technique by switching the subject. "Now, let me tell you a little bit about myself." Not wanting to have the minister forget the business objectives, I literally summed up the biographical sketch by saying, "I joined the company to become the general manager of ABC's intended subsidiary . . . you know, I previously lived in the Orient in Japan, which experience prompted me to consider another tour. Furthermore, I am presently charged with the responsibility to make the decision of where to locate the plant, with options of China *or* Korea, Hong Kong, Penang, Singapore, or Taiwan."

My last statement achieved the desired effect, although I did not appear to ruffle his feathers. He remained poised and began the bargaining for position by saying, "Mr. Tai Le, after listening to your outline of objectives, I have reached two major conclusions. First, that your company's objectives would fit well into our future plans for development of the electronics industry, although we are reluctant to encourage many more 'labor-intensive' investment projects. I like your company's 'family' concept of management. It fits well within our Chinese philosophy of 'family.' Secondly, I feel that your company's choice of general managers was an excellent one, and I would consider you as a welcome addition to our country. I feel you would work well with the Chinese people. So, let's say we have a mutual interest on which to develop the basis for our evaluation of your investment." Smiling, he tried on my understanding of

Chinese, asking for a positive indication of interest, by saying, "Hao bu hao?" Wanting to seal a bond of trust and friendship, I responded with the traditional Chinese "thumbs up" OK sign and a "Tseng Hsien Sheng, Ding Hao."

To his obvious satisfaction, he called for his secretary to have Lawrence Li come to his office. Lawrence Li, looking like the typical academic scholar, impeccable in his dress, his glasses highlighting my surface observation of a mild-mannered gentleman, was introduced by Minister Tseng. "Mr. Tai Le, I would like to have you meet, as you Americans say, my right-hand man, the executive secretary of our Investment Commission." After a warm, elbow-grabbing handshake, the minister continued by directing Mr. Li, first in Chinese and then by a translation for my benefit, "Please make yourself available to Mr. Tai Le and Mr. Chao, at their convenience, to completely review the outline of ABC's investment proposal. Mr. Tai Le is leaving in a few days to return to his US corporate headquarters to present his recommendations for a 'go-no go' decision." Then directing his attention to me, he concluded, "Mr. Tai Le, I have authorized Mr. Li to make direct, gentleman's commitments to you. On the surface of our conversation, I see no problems, except perhaps the request for market privilege. However, we want to explore this further with you. I hope you understand our concern is not to prevent you from entering our market, but for us to encourage development of our own local investment sources and protect the small entrepreneurial enterprises."

As if giving some final instructions to Mr. Li, he began to speak in Chinese. I could tell he was enjoying his role because he was beaming. When all three broke out in shades of boyish laughter, I realized that perhaps I was the focal point of the story. Interjecting my request over their laughter, "Minister, if it's not inappropriate, may I ask as to the nature of your humor at my expense?"

"You are right, Mr. Tai Le. It is not fair for us not to share our laughter with you. I have just related to Mr. Li and Mr. Chao the story about your predicament." Somewhat embarrassed, not realizing I had one, I asked, "What predicament?" Seriously, he answered, "Your sex-retary." After my initial blush, I joined all three of them in a second, hearty round of laughter, after which Minister Tseng kiddingly, but sincerely, indicated, "I've instructed Lawrence to help find you the right combination person, if you insist on following through with your American custom of hiring a female secretary. Chinese custom, although bending somewhat in recent years, permits only a man to hold an executive secretary's position, so as to promote maximum work efficiency and yet not create any source of temptation between the boss and subordinate relationship."

As we left, the minister generated a final round of chuckles when he privately spoke to Mr. Li in a questioning way, "Do you know Lotus Blossom?" Both Mr. Li's and my flush face gave him the answer, to which he added a stern, in a humorous, command, "Li Hsien Sheng, make sure she can also take dictation and type."

We all had a good round of laughter, and as I left his office with Mr. Li and Henry, I had to comment, "He sure leaves one with a feeling of having achieved a satisfactory understanding based on mutual interest and trust."

Mr. Li reinforced my impressions by saying, "Minister Tseng is very sincere," and furthered that feeling by asking, "Can we meet now in my office? I am anxious to resolve our interests to your satisfaction."

And within the hour, we had laid all the groundwork such that I was convinced that China was the right place for us. Like his boss, Mr. Li too was a man of action.

CHAPTER 10

A Royal Dinner and After?

Back at the hotel, comfortably sitting in the Dragon Bar, sipping on a scotch and water, I found myself reflecting on the future of my forthcoming experiences in China. The Chinese people I'd met so far, I liked. Industrious, warm, and sincere in character, I knew that they also possessed, in general, those important personal qualities of humor and love of life. A special feeling of satisfaction grew within me when I thought about the many pleasant memories that would be ours to share and enjoy. Suffice it to say . . . I was sold on the Chinese.

Departing from my reverie, and returning to reality, I glanced at my watch to note that it was after six, and I had a seven o'clock dinner engagement with the people from the Tenth Commercial Bank. In the few minutes interim period between the bar and my room, I received a smile and greetings of the day from no less than three of the hotel's employees. Not only had they succeeded in making me feel welcome as a guest, I now felt almost as if I were at home with them.

Promptly at seven o'clock, after a quick shave and change of clothes, the room phone rang. Peter Huang was asking if I were ready and instructing me to meet the party group in the lobby of the Mandarin Palace dining room. Within minutes, I was being introduced by Peter Huang, the manager, International Department, in the pecking order to Mr. Chiao, the chairman, to whom I had talked several days before. Next came Mr. Tu, Messrs. Wang and Lin of the downtown branch and Messrs. Ho and Fung of the Li branch. After the round of introductions, all the names became a blur, and I resolved right then to develop the habit of asking for a repeat at each future introduction. Perhaps, I thought that as my understanding of Chinese became better, that I could develop a true name-face association recall.

We were ushered into a small anteroom elevated above the main dining room, and everybody was seated again in the pecking order. My place was between the chairman and the president. Fortunately, Peter, whose English-speaking ability was good, sat close enough to stimulate and translate the conversation. All of the others expressed considerable reluctance in using their English.

Within seconds of our having been seated, the waitresses began to serve a choice of beer, Hsiao Shing and cokes. I chuckled to see the familiar sight of Coca-Cola, Pepsi, and R. C. Cola being offered. The drinking ritual got a quick start with the first welcome toast being offered by the esteemed chairman, Mr. Chang, who spoke in Chinese. "Huan Ying, Tai le Hsien Sheng. Gam Bei, a?" After a down-the-hatch, I felt obligated to offer a counter-toast, saying, "Let me express my thanks for the invitation and the pleasure of establishing this social relationship. Gam Bei, a?" With an obvious amusement at my use of Chinese, we all chugalugged a second glass of Hsiao Shing. At the pouring of a third round, a few faces began to flush and many of the subordinates turned their glasses upside down to signal their desire to switch to Coke. The chairman and president, however, who obviously had answered the challenge of many toasts in their lifetime, accepted their refills with obvious gusto, especially when I indicated that I was up to the "sport" and accepted a third round. They weren't about to "lose face" with an Occidental guest.

Drinking activities soon slowed down to a normal take-a-sip pace, permitting us to look at the menus, and also gave me a chance to look around. The decor of this large room, seating several hundred, was done in classical Chinese style done in teak wood paneling with many wood carvings and sculpturing. It left its guests with a feeling of warmth and elegance. In the center of the main dining room was a bandstand and in the forefront a parquet wood dance floor. I felt the presence of a small dance combo stage, however, rather incongruous in this setting, and I'm glad that my hunch was wrong as I saw a group of Chinese musicians, in their Imperial Palace floor-length blue Chinese gowns, each with a strange-looking instrument, sit down and begin to play some traditional Chinese music. Again, the mood was set for an enjoyable evening.

Peter interrupted my visions of the days of the dynasties by asking me, "Do you have any special preferences for dishes? Mr. Chiao would like to order, so we can be served before the show starts." Perusing the menu quickly, the memory of the Yellow Fish in sweet and sour sauce at the Grand Hotel jogged my taste buds, so I suggested, "If it suits everyone else, I'd like to try the Yellow Fish dish, and I'll defer to Mr. Chiao for his choice on the other dishes." The translation of my choice prompted a response of approval from several of the men at the table and a "Ding hao" from Mr. Chiao.

Shortly after the chairman finished the lengthy, well-calculated process of ordering, the procession of courses began. Just like the other meals before, the more they brought, the better they got. Before each dish, I was subjected to the usual round of Gam bei's by successive members of the party. Then, it dawned on me that I was drinking eight times more than the others as they each individually, rather than collectively, were drinking up. When my comment "You gentlemen are ganging up on me and trying to put a 'tiger' in my tank," was translated, they all laughed so loud and hard that heads from ten tables around turned to see what was going on. Just to make sure that everyone looking on would understand that I was not going to be the victim of their game, I stood up and said, "Gambie," with gusto and motioned for all of them to drink up, which they did, as I showed them my empty glass.

Shortly after, a large round dish of what looked like dumplings appeared on the table. Mr. Tu, who had been very quiet up till now, explained with Peter's help that these Chiao-tse were a favorite dish of people from northern China around his native province, the capital, Peiping. They were dipped into a small dish of vinegar and soy sauce and eaten out of a spoon with the aid of the chopsticks. They were delicious, and I couldn't adequately express myself, in Chinese, to let Mr. Tu know that I liked them, so I repeated after Peter that they, "the Chiao Tse" were "Hen hao chr!" Mr. Tu continued with his historical sketch to say, "In Northern China, Chiao Tse are often served as the only main dish, and that the guest must prepare to eat a minimum of fifty or cause grave 'loss of face' to the host. Many persons fast for several days before to develop an appropriate appetite, and often a game to see who can eat the most takes place. Often, after the contest, the competitors would rest for several days before eating again. There are reports of persons having eaten 100 or more." Everyone continued to listen intensely as I related, "The Americans have similar contests at our county fairs, with the contestants eating fruit pies with an added twist that no one can use his hands." They all laughed as Peter translated the "one-ups-manship" tale and the picture of this contest was mentally visualized. As the final stages of our marathon-eating contest came to an end, the lights dimmed, and the tempo of the music picked up, when a troupe of girls dressed in traditional Chinese gowns and costumes came out onto the dance floor. Each was a portrait of classical Oriental beauty . . . graceful in motion, doll-like in size, and alluring in looks, despite the white-paint face makeup. The music and their motions flowed together, as they performed a sequence of dances depicting the fateful lovers, the Emperor and Empress, the rice harvest, and the Dragon and the Phoenix stories of classic literature. All of the cosmetics put together, the room, the food, the music, and the entertainment gave one exactly the feeling that the evening was intended to inspire. I imagined myself as the Emperor enjoying the comforts of life in the Mandarin Palace of the Imperial Dynasties.

Too soon, the show and meal were over although it was already 9:30. I breathed a sigh of relief, when Mr. Chiao and company all got up and we shook hands to say, "Thanks, good night, and we'll talk again on Monday to learn of your decision." Peter, too, after taking me to look at the Chinese string, wind and bell instruments of the orchestra, then left me at the entrance of the door, saying, "Mr. Tai Le, I'd like to suggest that we call this a complete evening. I would enjoy taking you to other entertainment spots in tonight, but we Chinese feel that an evening of classical entertainment should not be spoiled by mixture of other more base forms." "Peter," I said, looking forward to a few hours to myself, "I agree with your philosophy, completely. Thanks for the evening of cultural exposure. I'll call you on Monday."

Feeling very relaxed and free for the rest of the evening, I decided that I'd go back to the room, read a little, work on my weekly report, and listen to some soft music before turning in for a good evening's sleep.

As I got off the elevator on the fifth floor to go to my room, Walter extended a cheerful hello and asked, "Mr. Tai Le, you plan to stay in your room now?" To which I answered, "Yes." "You go to sleep now?" To which I responded, "No." "You relax, then," he responded, almost with a half statement, half question to the tone of his voice I thought to myself as I entered the room that it was nice of him to express his personal concern.

I was enjoying the moment of relaxation, and a couple of hours slipped by. I enjoyed a chuckle out of rereading my front page ad in the *China Post*, as well as the news of the day, wondering what the ad would look like tomorrow morning. Writing my report and listening to the mood music of the "China Watch" program on the AFRT radio channel piped into the console in the room, intermixed with a sprinkling of news on the hour, took me up to midnight and a decision to hit the sack.

Just as I finished leaving a morning call for 8:00 a.m., there was a quiet, but distinct knock on my door. Waltzing to the door in my pajamas, I opened the door to look face-to-face at Walter. He stood there rigid, hands to his side, and stammered a little, as if with embarrassment. "Mr. Tai Le, are you OK?" "Yes," I said, suspicious now of his concern. Somewhat chagrined, he continued, "I see your light on, and I worry if you are sick."

"Why?" I asked. "It is now four nights you stay in my room, and you not have a girl in your room yet to sleep with." "Walter," I said, "I am feeling very well. I just have much work to do and no time to play." Puffing up his chest, he stated emphatically, "Old Chinese proverb, spoken by Confucius, say, 'All work and no play, make man a dull boy.'" And at that, he stepped aside to unveil his present to me, the cute little bar girl that had been tempting me each time I passed the Butterfly Club down the road from the hotel. She stepped up to me and looked up at me with a soulful look, to ply her charms, saying, "I know you not happy. How about you let me make you happy? I like to stay with you." Then she added, "No charge."

Somewhat angered over the setup, somewhat embarrassed standing there in my BVDs, and somewhat tempted to accept the offer, I had to think quickly on my feet. Apologetically, I began, "Walter, I appreciate your thoughts for my welfare and happiness . . . and you, young lady, tonight is now tomorrow morning, and I have to get up early. As much as I would enjoy your company for the evening, I do not think that it is fair for you to keep my friend waiting at the Butterfly Club." Walter, as her interpreter, asked, "What friend you mention?" Seriously, I fibbed, "I talked to my friend Bill Lorris just a few minutes ago on the phone. He was looking for an evening of pleasure, and I suggested to him that he visit this young lady for some companionship at the Butterfly Club. He must be there now looking for her." With that, Walter, the procurer, and his friend backed away from the door saying, in unison, "Thank you, Mr. Tai Le . . . Hsieh Hsieh Ni!" Both were quickly off to the elevators to make sure she . . . and probably Walter . . . didn't miss on the profit opportunity. "Ah yes," I thought, as I closed the door. "Close call on my chastity, and wow, these Chinese entrepreneurial instincts!"

CHAPTER 11

Getting the Job Search "Right"?

Expecting to sleep in late again was too much to ask for. The cacophony of horns of taxis, cars, and the busses in and unbelievable traffic jam at the front of the hotel was too much to escape from ... even after ducking my head under the pillow.

Angry at first, when I looked at my watch to find it was only 8:30 in the morning, my temperament changed to one of humor as I looked out the window down on the entanglement. There must have been fifty-nine vehicles within a space of one block, in fifty-nine different positions other than in their respective lanes of traffic, and the situation wasn't getting better as others bullied their way into the fracas. I chuckled as I imagined the frustration that such a predicament would bring to a police man from NYC in unsnarling the combatants and the satisfaction that it would bring as he ticketed the violations of the traffic rules.

As the novelty of the bumper-to-bumper conflict wore off, I remembered that today was the day of reckoning my ad in the *China Post*, so I eagerly retrieved the copy from under my room door. Sure enough, the new ad, on the front page, had been corrected and now appeared very proper in its bold format:

ABC, a U.S. Electronics Firm
needs
an Executive Secretary

At the bottom of the ad was an editor's footnote apology in italics:

Correction: The editor wishes to apologize to Mr. R. Tai Le for the typographical error in previous copy and clarify. Mr. Tai Le wants to hire a talented person who is highly proficient in secretarial skills. But, he will not, he has explained, refuse to hire a female who combines these skills with beauty.

"Well put," I acknowledged out loud, although I wasn't too happy at being exposed personally, by name, to the whole world.

Knowing that the only thing I was committed to accomplish, until my dinner appointment with Cecil and the Hwa Chang Bank people, was personal, to do some house hunting, take a look at the school, and shop around for a car. I decided to sit down and leisurely read through the "For Sale or Rent" ads in the *China Post*.

After scanning the ads, I decided that 1. I'd better look for the professional assistance of a realtor since I didn't know the territory and 2. that I ought to get some new car buyer's help from an authorized agency to get some base of reference facts on prices for comparison before shopping on the used car market.

The ad on VW's—new and used—caught my attention immediately, so I made a quick call. The answer on the other end "Wei" by a weak, feminine voice threw me for a curve, but I continued on asking, "Is the sales manager in?" "Please to hold a minute" was the shaky answer with a definite trace of courtesy expressed with an Oriental's insecurity in the English language. I waited, what seemed to be an eternity, which was only thirty seconds, while listening to a definite undertone of giggling between the switchboard operator and another female until a man picked up the phone, saying, "Hello, Mr. Fung speaking. What can I do for you?" Again, I responded, "I would love to speak with the sales manager about some prices on a new V.W." Proudly, he responded, "Sales manager speaking. Please to give your name, address, and phone number. I will send salesperson to your office right now." "Mr. Fung," I say, "I am Tai Le." Interrupting, he asked, "Please to spell." "Tai Le Hsien Sheng," I said in my best Chinese. "Very good, I see you speak Chinese," he complimented. Resuming again, I said, "I am staying at Tong Yi Da Fa Tien in room 508 and am available at any time before 5:00 p.m. today to talk with your representative." "Hen hao le!" he exclaimed. "I send her to the hotel room right now." And at that instant, the phone conversation came to an end.

Picking up the paper again to scan the houses for sale or rent ads, I spotted a realtor ad that almost read as if it were composed by an American:

> "A House Should Be A Man's Castle"
> To see the best in Grass Mountain,
> Tien Mou and Peitou
> Call Lodge Right—Day or Night
> Phone 88-3344

The response to my call convinced me that I must be dealing with an American. "Good morning, this is Lodge Right speaking. May I be of assistance to you?" After introducing myself, as Tai Le and recapping all the specifics of my forthcoming assignment as general manager of ABC, I proceeded to detail my requirements. "Lodge, I would like to find a four-bedroom home with a little land, preferably away from the Little America compounds. Do you know Barry Frazier of the BICF bank?" I asked. "Sure do," was his response. "Well," I explained, "if you could find me a place like his in the setting I described, I'd like to see it." "If I don't have it, I can find it for you. What is your schedule today?" he asked. "I should have the afternoon free until 5:00 p.m." "Good," he responded. "Would you like to meet me at the Foremost Dairy Shop in Tien Mou for lunch at 12:30?" Immediately, sensing a free lunch, which by nature of my conservatism, I never turn down, I responded, "Half past twelve, I'll catch a taxi and meet you there." "See you later," was the end of conversation, and we both hung up. "Gee," I thought to myself, "it'll be great dealing with a Westerner, who knows what an American's specifications for a house really are."

Putting our own "Teahouse of the August Moon," in my mind, must have consumed at least fifteen minutes before I snapped back to reality, realizing that if Mr. Fung meant what he said about sending someone immediately, I'd better get the lead out and get shaved, showered, and dressed before I got involved in any business discussions. Somehow, I couldn't really imagine myself making a deal in my pajamas.

Fortunately, I got my hygienic duties accomplished, because just as I was finishing, I heard a knock on the door. Imagine my surprise when I find myself standing face-to-face with Grace, who introduced herself in perfect English, "Good morning, Mr. Tai Le. My name is Grace Wang. I'm the sales representative for VW of Taiwan." Before I could regain a state of normal composure, because I frankly must admit, she was really a remarkably beautiful woman, who was very calmly asking, "May I come in so we can discuss business?" Looking out the door into the hallway, I saw a beaming Walter, the floor boy, giving me the "thumbs up" sign of approval. As I resigned myself to giving up my perfect reputation as an "untouchable," I attempted to recover by a defensive maneuver, asking, "Miss Wang, wouldn't you be more comfortable talking over a cup of coffee or some breakfast in the Coffee Shop downstairs?" Responding without batting an eye, she obviously wasn't the least bit concerned for her moral safety when she answered, "If you would like, but," she emphasized, "don't feel like it's necessary on my account, since I've already had my breakfast, and I really think we can accomplish much more right here in your room." I didn't quite know how she was intending her "much more" phrase, but before I could make a Boy Scout "morally straight" decision, I let her in.

Once she was past the threshold, she left the initiation of conversation up to me, as she walked to take a look out of the window. Boy . . . the thoughts that were going through my mind! It's funny how adrenalin flows when one is in a compromising situation. Bound and determined to keep the relationship on a no-monkey business plan, I started the conversation and got my faux pas only after I'd said, "OK, Miss Wang, show me what you've got." She looked at me straight in the eye, and if she understood my poor choice of words, she didn't let on as she efficiently, but in a lady-like fashion, sat down and opened her briefcase to hand me some sales literature. "I have here a complete library of catalogs to show you our VW Beetle, 411, Variant and Micro-bus product lines." As I looked at them and asked a number of questions, it was obvious she didn't know much about cars. Her stock answer was always stated in an honest, but beguiling way, without embarrassment. "I'm sorry, Mr. Tai Le, I do not know the answer to your question, but if it isn't answered in the brochure, I can surely get an answer for you at the office." I'm sure you can appreciate that it took some time to finally boil this "cat and mouse" questions and no-answers session down to a specification for a Variant Station Wagon, with straight shift, 1700 CC engine, beige exterior and interior trim colors, with air-conditioning, etc. "Now, can you price my specification?" I asked. Again, very sweetly, but businesslike, she answered, "Mr. Tai Le, I can't do the pricing of an order. Mr. Fung is the only one who can do that, but I'd be happy to get you an answer from the office." "OK," I said. "How long will that take?" No sooner than I'd asked, she replied, "Mr. Tai Le, may I use your phone to call the office?" As soon as I'd said, "Sure, please use the phone over there by the bed," she was dialing for Mr. Fung.

Her entire conversation with Mr. Fung took place in Chinese, interrupted occasionally by a question to me in English. As soon as she'd finished, she said, "Mr. Fung will have a pro forma for you by noon. Now, Mr. Tai Le, would you like to take a test drive?" Thinking that this would be an excellent opportunity for me to try my skill in competition with the world's best "kamikaze" pilots, I responded with an immediate, "Yes, let's go."

As we both walked out of the room, engaged in social conversation, I noticed the glance and smile of approval from Walter. His final vote of confidence was cast in his farewell statement as Grace and I entered the elevator. "Sure glad you not sick anymore, Mr. Tai Le. Please to have a fine day."

In the elevator, Grace turned to me and apologized without embarrassment, "Mr. Tai Le, I'm sorry that I have not been able to be a good salesperson to you. Maybe you will understand my problem. I have been a salesperson only three months and drove a car for the first time only two months ago. But I want to learn, so I can be the best VW salesperson in China. You seem to know much about cars. Would you help me learn more?"

No one could refuse a plea as sincere as Grace's, especially from a pretty and determined young lady like her. So, when she offered the keys to me, as we approached the little Beetle across the street, I said, "Grace, let's see if you drive as well as your determination to be the No. 1 saleslady." So, taking my life into my own hands, I climbed into the car and jokingly said, "Grace, in the States, we call this the suicide seat. What do you call it in Chinese?" Composed, but hurt by my question, she replied, "Mr. Tai Le, don't be frightened. I am a very good driver." And as we proceeded down the street and onto Chung Shan North road, it was obvious that she was. Traveling over some excellent roads, we were quickly out of the city and into the suburban area. The sun was shining, and the sky was robin-egg blue, without a cloud in sight. A light breeze was blowing through the car's open windows, and I can honestly say I was enjoying this ride more than any other I'd had in Japan and/or China.

Grace was driving very well, and we engaged nonchalantly in some sightseer's conversation as she called my attention to the village of Shihlin. She slowed down as we encountered at least five hundred lovelies leaving and or coming to Ming Chuan Girl's college. Then she directed my attention to the GMO's residential palace nestled back off the road at the base of a mountain. Shortly after we came upon a stoplight, I spotted a Foremost Dairy Store. I asked, "Is this the Foremost Store in Tien Mou?" Answering with a quick "Yes," she continued on saying, "Our showroom is just over the bridge straight ahead." Then coming back to my question, she asked, "Mr. Tai Le, if you do not feel this is improper, may I ask you to join me for lunch after we finish talking to Mr. Fung?" "Grace, even though our movies may have taught you that it's the man's place to invite a lady, that's old-fashioned. I'd be very honored to have lunch with you, but I've already promised someone that I'd meet him for lunch at Foremost's. But, maybe you'd be willing to give me a rain check for another time?" At that, we pulled into the entrance for a very modern and impressive showroom, advertised plainly as VW. As Grace parked, she turned and looked at me with a quizzical look. "It is not raining, so what is a rain check?" No sooner than we had parked, and without adequate time for me to explain the "rain check" acceptance of her invitation, Mr. Fung was opening my door and introducing himself. "I, Mr. Fung. So happy to meet you. Please to come in my office." Mr. Fung was certainly an eager business man, and he lost no time pursuing an order. "Mr. Tai Le, it is no good to buy a used car now. Used car is costing more than new one. Cars in great demand; here our country." He explained, "You lucky person. Foreign businessman who live in China have privilege to import one car. Chinese persons—not so. Most buy used if they want now, or buy a government import permit. Only two thousand given each year, people wait three years or more to get approved. So, if you buy a new, then after six months, you can sell for 50 percent profit. Used car—US make—you buy from military is very expensive. You have to pay car price the 125 percent of car value, when new, as import duty. Two-year-old car will cost you US$12,000, may be US$15,000. I can sell you new VW 150cc Station Wagon for only $10,000."

A little hesitant that I was getting a quick sell, I said, "Mr. Fung, sounds like you know what you are talking about, but I'd just like to have you give me a quotation today. I'm not ready to make a decision yet. I don't need the car for at least two to two and half months." Quickly, but not offensively, he jumped back on the sales attack. "If you order me today, I have new car here for you by July 15. If you wait, one more week later, next delivery is September."

Well, I survived the high-pressure tactics and felt like I was lucky to escape with just a quotation in my hand, vowing to do some double-checking before I committed. Grace walked out with me, her voice almost apologetic from Mr. Fung's assault, "Mr. Tai Le, if you decide to buy VW, I hope you will buy from me." "Grace," I assured her, "I wouldn't buy it from anybody else. I promise." With my promise, her face lit up with a beautiful smile and said, "You will be my best customer." Then, changing the subject, she asked, "Can I drive you down to the Foremost?" Looking at my watch, I noticed I still had fifteen minutes to meet Mr. Lodge Right, so I said, "No, thanks. It's not that far, and it's a great day, so I'd enjoy the walk. Hao bu hao?" Still smiling, she gave me a Chinese OK answer "Hao" and a cute "Dzai Jen, Dzai Jen."

Chapter 12

Finding the "Right" House

The walk from the VW showroom was quick and most enjoyable. The view from the bridge gave me my first opportunity to really stop and look over the sights of the suburbia in China. I spotted a Chinese temple which sat high up on a monolith. To the back of me, in about a 270-degree semicircle, rose a soft green, lush, not too rugged set of mountains, and smack in the center two large block letter Chinese characters that were clearly visible for miles on a clear day. About a third of the way up the mountain, a large complex of majestic buildings in traditional pagoda, swept-roof Chinese architecture . . . . Glancing at my watch, I noticed I'd stopped to look almost too long, and that I was going to be late if I didn't hurry up, but I found it difficult to tear myself away from this quiet, pastoral landscape. I promised myself that I'd have to explore some of these interesting sights soon.

I walked the remaining two block's distance past many interesting shops, selling everything from pets to rattan furniture before I came to the Foremost Dairy Store. The store was actually a dairy bar and short order restaurant that would have passed for a spot I used to frequent in my high school days back in Moline, Illinois . . . It was crowded with lunch-time customers, most of them young boys and girls, both Chinese and Occidentals, looking like they were of high school and college age. Luckily,

I found one vacant table right by a large window that looked out toward one of the two main streets. I found myself content to look out at the traffic and the activity at the service station across the street, which was busy pumping gas for a collection of vehicles like I'd never seen before, including motorcycles, motorized three-wheel trucks, cabs, busses, trucks, as well as an occasional passenger car. It wasn't long before I noticed a very handsome young man in a business suit, looking like a Chinese Tab Hunter. It was obvious that he was in a hurry, as he pulled up on a motorcycle, got off looking at his watch, and came into the store. I watched him as he looked around and then he walked up to my table. "You must be Mr. Tai Le." I acknowledged, "Yes, I am." He proceeded to introduce himself, saying, "Please accept my apologies for being late. I'm Lodge Right. May I join you?" I thought to myself, "If this young man is as good as his first impressions, we ought to have a fruitful day."

"How long have you been in China?" he asked. "Have you had a chance to do some house-hunting before now? Can you tell me a little about your family and what kind of housing needs, likes and dislikes you have?" Summarizing, he said, "This type of information will give me a better idea of what to look at, rather than waste your time looking at houses and/or locations that wouldn't be of interest to you."

Somewhere in between our conversation to lay the groundwork for our exploring expedition, we ordered lunch. "Had a lot of Chinese meals lately?" When I answered, "Yes," he responded with a question-suggestion, "How'd you like a *good*, old-fashioned American hamburger to give you some variety in your diet?" He was smiling, knowing that my answer would be a quizzical, "Why? Yes! Here?" Lodge put his seal of fine cooking recommendation forth. "They have the best hamburger sandwich here in China, even better than the 'O' Club. Try one." So I did, and I placed my order to a very wholesome-looking teenage waitress, just like back home (except that she was Chinese). "I'll have a hamburger and a chocolate milkshake."

We talked as we ate, mostly Lodge telling me about the housing situation. "The three main 'expatriate' housing areas are on Yangmingshan, also known as Grass Mountain, Peitou, and Tien Mou. You're coming at a good time of year. Many houses are now available or will be shortly, as most of the turnover occurs during the months of May through August, when the school year is over and businessmen's families are transferred. I can show some houses that I think will suit your needs. Let's finish here and then grab a cab up to my office on the Mountain, where I can show you some pictures of what I have to offer. Of course, I know of a few more that are under construction that should be ready by August, when you come back with your family. By the way," he concluded, "how was the hamburger, as good as home cooking?"

"Fantastic," was just about the only way I could express myself. "In fact, I'd have to admit that it was almost as good as my own charcoal grilled or barbecued." "Barbeque!" exclaimed Lodge. "Do you like barbeque?" Before I could answer, he had a proposition. "Tell you what, Tai Le . . ." he paused for a second and then said, "May I address you as Tai Le? If you treat for lunch, I'll treat for dinner. If you like the barbecue, I know you'll like a Chinese smorgasbord. It will take us the rest of the afternoon to look at some houses. We'll start on the Mountain, then come down the back way to Peitou, and then finish up in Tien Mou." "Sounds great to me! Is this the same type of barbecue as they serve up at the 'O' Club?" I asked. "The barbecue you refer to is Mongolian-style cooking. The smorgasbord I am taking you to is a Chinese street vendor style, but I really think you will enjoy this food even better," was Lodge's answer. "OK," I said, acknowledging my acceptance of his invitation. "By the way," he asked, "would you mind if I bring along my wife?" "I'd be honored to dine in the company of a lady," I formally answered. "If she's anything like you, she has to be some woman." "Thank you," was his sole reply. "I'll introduce you to Karen, who is not only my partner for life, but also the better half of my business. She shows all the lady clients around."

I paid the very reasonable tab of RMB$97, about $10.40, as Lodge went out to catch a taxi. I couldn't help but thinking to myself, "If this fellow's housing recommendations are as good as his taste in clothes, command of the English language, and a meal choice that really hit the spot, I knew we'd find the right place for the Tai Le family."

As we climbed into the taxi, I was worried that he'd forgotten his motorcycle. "No," he replied, "it'll be all right, right where it is. I'll pick it up on our way back from the smorgasbord tonight, since it'll be right on our way home." One other thought came to my mind as we headed toward the Mountain. "Lodge, one other condition on this house project. I'd like to stay away from living in one of the 'Little America' housing compounds I've heard about. We'd prefer to find a place that is out in the rice paddies, if possible." "I know of a couple places that might suit your interests, but let's take a representative look, OK?" he answered.

I liked this young man's answer. He knew when to lead the conversation and when to let me take the initiative or simply settle for silence to let his comments and/or the scenery sink in . . . and that he did as the little cab began to chug up the mountain and wind around some of the curves exposing some of the most beautiful panoramic views of the river basin, the plains, and the rice fields below. As we wound our way, cork-screw fashion, up the beautiful roadway of tropical trees and lined with bushes covered with flowers, one could almost feel we were going to enter a state of heavenly serenity. Within ten minutes, we were at the Lodge Right office. Although the scenery had been most pleasant, I was glad to get out of the cab, as I was afraid the driver was going to tear the engine and transmission to pieces trying to accomplish these 15-20 percent mountain grades in third gear, but I realized I was in for some more of the same as he told the driver in Chinese to wait.

The office was very plain-looking and small from a first glance from the outside. It was small on the inside, but very functional, and graced by the charm of a very lovely young lady looking very business-like and who happened to be on the phone. Lodge beaming with pride, nudged me, gestured at her, and whispered, "My wife, Karen." He didn't waste a minute getting to work as he went to a bookcase and selected three big books labelled Yangmingshan, Peitou, and Tien Mou. He opened the books, and suggested that I sit down, and proposed in offering me one of the books that I glance through the pictures and specifications he had compiled on each house that he had to show. "Why don't you look at these and pick out two or three in each area for us to look at this afternoon?" he said. It was obvious from his organization that he'd learned from someone the psychology of American realtor's show and tell tactics.

As soon as she was off the phone, Lodge took the initiative with a great deal of pride to introduce me. "Karen, this is Mr. Tai Le." She really radiated personal charm as she responded, "Mr. Tai Le, welcome to our humble, little office. Lodge has mentioned your conversation to me, and I hope we can help you find a house that you and your family will enjoy. I have made notes on several houses that I think might be right for your family needs. After you have finished looking through our pictures, then let me compare my choices with yours." Within ten to fifteen minutes, I had picked out six prospects and was amazed to find that she had picked five out of the six that I had selected. "Believe me, my 'blind ad' pick confidence has sure been rewarded," I said. Humbly, Lodge replied, "Not until we have found you a 'RIGHT' house." Karen, laughingly, said, "Please excuse our play on words, Mr. Tai Le."

With that, Lodge had taken the six pictures and word descriptions and we were back in the taxi. After giving instructions to the driver in Chinese, he said, "Now that I have a fair idea of what you want, I'd like to show you what you've picked and then show you a few others that I have in mind." The next four hours we spent driving up small lanes, climbing in and out of the taxi, and evaluating the factors of neighborhoods, number of rooms, floor plans, interior decor, views, rental costs, etc. We went from a house in the middle of 'Little America' to the rice boondocks, from not enough space to houses that would only be right for an embassy, from no interior decor tastes to some that looked like a palace, from rentals of US $200 to $1,000 per month, and frankly, I was getting discouraged. "Lodge," I said, "maybe I am expecting too much, but I just haven't seen the house yet that gives me the 'RIGHT' feeling, if I can use your name as a play on words." Sensing that I was weary of the inspection tour, he said, putting his arm around my shoulder, in consolation, "Let's take a look at one last place in Tien Mou. It's still under construction, but I think it could be finished in time, if we negotiate." Lodge told the driver to turn off the main road, and for the first time all day, I finally had a feeling that we were in China. The narrow road wound its way past many small open shops, selling fruits, vegetables, meats, hardware, and the local neighborhood noodle shop, and then out into the rice fields. The road began to bend along the outline of a small creek full of water, probably coming off the mountain, which was the main source of water for irrigating the fields. The fields were alive with activity. Men and women were busy hoeing, standing in the rice paddies up to their knees in mud. Others were skimming a green, seedy substance off the ponds of water lotus plants. There were also many people tending to small vegetable garden patches and commercial flower gardens.

All of the sudden, Lodge asked the taxi driver to stop by a small roadside general store. Here, he ordered a bottle of cola for each of the three of us. Although it was warm, it tasted great, but more than anything, it gave me a real opportunity to get out and look at a countryside that was really what I expected and wanted to see and enjoy in living in a part of China.

We climbed back into the taxi and continued along this picturesque little one-way road to 'Shangrila' without a word being spoken. We turned off the small road onto even a more narrow lane and proceeded to go up a slight incline at the base of the mountain. There were small farm houses nestled in the safety of the coves and niches of this rocky, but tropically lush area. As we approached the top of the upgrade, a large combination brick and stone house of Western contemporary architecture emerged into our view. Although it was unfinished, it gave off the impression of being a diamond in the rough. In front was a large lagoon with a number of Chinese gazebo buildings surrounded by flowers. The house was situated within four walls on about an acre of land, terraced with gardens of bamboo and many varieties of tropical fruit trees and flowers. Off to the side of the house, where workmen were building a swimming pool, there stood a cabana made of *bamboo*. "I can just visualize the pleasure of living in a setup like this, but isn't this place likely to be super-expensive?" I asked. "Let's go inside and see if we can see the owner," suggested Lodge.

There must have been fifteen workmen, all busily engaged in the process of finishing the interior. After asking several workmen, we finally were directed upstairs to find the owner, a Mr. Tze. As we climbed the shape of a circular staircase, I fully expected to meet an elderly man but was completely surprised when we introduced ourselves to a very handsome, short, but well-built man with a firm handshake who was no more than thirty-five. Mr. Tze spoke very little English, but it was clear that he was very proud of this architectural masterpiece which he was building. He took us out on the balcony to look out over *his* next-door house, and he had every right to be proud. The setting was beautiful. Remembering T.C's description of the scenery from the Grand Hotel, I said in my poor Chinese, "Hen hao fun jing." His pleasure in my comment was obvious. I stood and looked out over the Tien Mou valley with its lush green fields and backdrop of majestic mountains. Walking around the balcony on the sides and back of the house, one could see every detail of the neighboring farm houses and their occupants working diligently in their well-ordered and meticulously kept terraced and irrigated gardens.

I hated to tear myself away from the scenery but had to complete my inspection of the house. With three thousand square feet of living space, five bedrooms, excellent kitchen facilities, servants' quarters, and a living room as big as some houses, I didn't have to debate whether or not it was adequate for our needs. We discussed his plans for finishing the house, and when he offered to allow me to help him choose the decorative items, the lighting, and asked for suggestions on the wiring, I came to the conclusion that Mr. Tze would be a most accommodating landlord. Mr. Tze, sensing my interest, asked, "Tai Le Hsien Sheng, you like to rent?" Fearful that it was beyond my means, I answered, "Mr. Tze, I am afraid it is too Tai Gway (too expensive)." To which he responded, "How much can you pay?" That sounded like he was shooting for the moon, so I said in a discouraging tone, "I cannot afford more than US$300 per month." Without so much as batting an eye, he said, "300, OK?" I thought for a while and then acknowledged, "OK." His immediate response was "You like to shake on a fair deal?" It was obvious that we both felt we got a bargain and proceeded to establish our agreement by almost shaking each other's arm off.

After resolving a few more details on when the house was to be ready, Lodge and I walked around the place one more time. I surveyed the house and yard like a king would survey his castle. The sun was setting beyond the mountains as we pulled away. Its warm orange glow left me with a feeling of complete satisfaction.

I knew as I looked back, as we pulled away in the taxi, that "Life in China for the Tai Le Family was going to start out 'RIGHT.'"

Chapter 13

Meals on Wheels

Lodge explained, as our taxi took us back to the Foremost Dairy store to meet the wife, Karen, "Our destination for dinner tonight is the Food Circle. Now, this is not going to be anything fancy like the restaurants in which you've been eating. In fact, it's outdoors. But this is really what eating out is like for most people in China."

After we picked up Karen, who was waiting for us, we took a twenty-minute taxi ride into several completely new sections of the city . . . at least, I hadn't seen them before. Each of the areas we drove through, the wholesale market, the housing tenements, and along the river, created new and fascinating sights. The streets and sidewalks were jammed packed with people, shopping, on their way home from work, and some just out for a stroll. "Lodge," I said, "you know I never cease to be amazed at how well-dressed and healthy the people look. I had imagined from all the past reports one has heard about China that there would be a lot of hunger and poverty." With pride, he responded, "Our government has done much to improve the welfare of the people, since the days of the revolution."

Karen picked up the cue to relate her feelings, "You know, Mr. Tai Le, many of the stories you hear we also have heard from our parents and others, but most of which are traceable to the days after the war when a great depression came over China.

Much of the country was still at war within itself and money became worthless. People had no jobs, there was much stealing and looting, and frankly, untold thousands of people died of hunger." Lodge continued, "I feel they have done a responsible job of satisfying the needs of the people. Perhaps the problems are more manageable now. We are grateful for our existence and constantly improving our standard of living. We have a great deal of hope for our future, despite the fact that most of the governments of the world have given up on political support for us."

At that, Lodge instructed the cab driver to pull over and stop. Dusk was now upon us, and the streets in front of us were lighted, on both sides, from the glow of hundreds of sidewalk carts and stalls. Their soft glow almost gave one the impression that the streets were lighted by a never-ending string of pearls.

"Welcome to the Food Circle, a Chinese gourmet's paradise," was Lodge's introduction, as we proceeded to walk down the street. Karen explained, as we walked, "Here you will find many different foods, gaming places, many dime-store items and clothing merchants, Shiao Shing wine stands, etc. The owners of these stands bring them in late in the afternoon, stay open for business until midnight, then close them up, and pull them home. For many, this represents what you Westerners call a 'moonlight' job."

Lodge suggested, "Let's walk the entire area. Then we'll decide what and where we'd like to eat."

We must have walked for at least forty-five minutes down one side of Chungking Road, and I was fascinated to see and smell the hundreds of different specialties being prepared right there before my eyes. No stall was any bigger than a space of ten feet by ten feet, with seating on wooden stools for maybe six to eight people. The selection ranged from Chinese noodle dishes to fried snake meat. You even get to pick your snake, like we pick a lobster out of a tank. The carts that were selling trinkets and clothes were fascinating to watch. The offer and sale of each item was based on the age-old custom of bargaining. The exchange of bidding and asking prices often prompted a seeming violent explosion of temper and threatening words, none of which I understood, but Karen explained, "In China, almost every purchase is bargained for. Most merchants would feel hurt if you didn't engage them in this round-robin event." She suggested, "You too, shouldn't hesitate to negotiate as soon as you learn a little of the language. If you can make a purchase for 50 percent or less of the original asking price, then consider that you've made a really good buy." When we had walked a little further, we came upon a stall that was selling some very nice jade jewelry pieces. I knew my wife would enjoy a jade bracelet or necklace, so with Karen's help, as my interpreter, we established the prices, piece by piece. She suggested a strategy, "Look at many things, and we'll ask the price. Don't pick up the one you really want until you've looked at several others you don't want. We'll bargain on each to let him know his prices are too high. Then, when we've got a good feeling for how much he's willing to negotiate on something we don't want, then we'll pick up the one you want and nail him down." I picked out a beautiful gold pendant necklace with a teardrop shaped jade stone. After looking at many other items, Karen agreed, "The quality of the stone looks good." We got an initial price of RMB$100, about US$12, and then told him it was too much. Karen told him, in Chinese, "It's only worth RMB$25." That made him angry. He ranted and raved, so she put it back, grabbed my arm, and said, "Let's walk away and see what happens. But, one thing, if you're not satisfied with his last asking price as we walk away, don't go back, or he'll know that he's hooked you." His counter offer was RMB$60, so she said, "Keep walking." As we did, he shouted another offer of RMB$50. "Let's stop," she said, "to let him know, we'll have to talk this over." "Karen," I said, "let's take it. Hell, I think it's a good buy at RMB$100, and I'd rather not haggle any more. I can afford it." Then she proceeded to give me a lecture. "OK," she said, "but let me explain something. Don't you forget that you're going to pay more just because you're an American, a Westerner... probably 25 percent more than a Chinese. If you give in to his asking price, or any other merchant, and then a few others do the same, he's going to think he can ask a higher price from Chinese as well. Little bit by little bit, he and all the other merchants will adjust their pricing-bargaining philosophy so that the common everyday Chinese person is going to have to pay more the next time he shops. So don't give up on bargaining for what you think is a fair price, even if you can afford to pay more. You'll see what I mean when you shop in the tourist shops on Chung Shan or the grocery stores in Tien Mou. In fact, when your wife comes, I hope I can show her how to save much money by shopping at the market places, rather than in the American and foreigner one-price expensive stores." I couldn't get a word of rebuttal in edgewise, until she finished, but I finally said, "For a very quiet and well-mannered young lady, you sure know how to get your message across."

The merchant's attitude changed to a broad grin and self-satisfied look, as he wrapped my first purchase, and when I handed him the RMB$50, he profusely thanked us, in Chinese, "Hsieh, Hsieh . . . Hsieh, Hsieh." As we walked away, she whispered, "Now, if I were alone and wanted to buy that necklace, I probably could have bought it for RMB$40." Then, she smiled and said, "But I'm happy that you're pleased and I hope your wife will be, too. It is a very pretty and well-made piece."

Resuming our shopping experience, we continued our walk down the street to look at other vendors' shops. Feeling some hunger pangs and smelling some very wonderful aromas, we spotted a very interesting food booth and stopped to look and sample taste. "This food stand with the Gi Bao Fan (Chicken vegetable rice casserole) looks great to me," said Lodge. "Shall we have some?" So, Lodge picked out three stools and ordered for all of us. The cook placed three sets of chopsticks and tea cups in front of us. Within five minutes, three dishes of what looked like a casserole were placed in front of us. Before I could pick up my chopsticks, Lodge was dipping all three pairs in a boiling hot water pot behind the counter. He recommended, as he sat down, "It is a good idea whenever you eat out in a place like this to make sure your eating utensils are properly sterilized. Well, . . . Chow." It sure was a simple dish, but the taste was excellent. "Hen hao chr," I said. Both the cook and Lodge answered, simultaneously, "Hsieh Hsieh Ni." It didn't look like a lot to eat, but halfway through, I paused to catch my breath. Not wanting to put my chopsticks down on the counter, I stuck them into the mound of rice, sticking straight up. Immediately, the cook became flushed and said something in Chinese to Lodge, who advised me, "Tai Le, Chinese people are very superstitious. I know you don't mean to offend anyone, so let me suggest that you don't ever leave your chopsticks like that. It is a bad omen. The symbol of chopsticks left in the rice bowl is only done at the time of a funeral. When a bowl of rice with chopsticks is placed on the coffin, it signifies that although the pleasure of life is over, it is hoped that the soul will have sufficient food to enjoy in the good life hereafter." The significance of what I had done came over me fast, and I asked Lodge, quietly as I removed the chopsticks, "How do I apologize to the cook?" Answering, he said, "Just a simple 'Dewi bu chi' will be adequate." So, I offered my apologies, saying, "Hsien Sheng, Dewi bu chi, dewi bu chi, a?" Then Lodge filled in with further apologies. Relieved, the cook soon returned to his pleasant self, humbly asking if the meal was acceptable. Reassured by me, as I completely emptied my bowl, Lodge ordered a second dish of Gi Bao Fan, (chicken and veggies over rice casserole) which we agreed to split. As we finished it also, the pleased look on the cook's face told me the embarrassment of the 'chopsticks' situation was forgiven and forgotten. I was amazed, as we walked away, and Lodge gave the vendor two RMB$50 bills that the meal had cost us less than what I had spent for lunch at the Foremost Dairy.

We finished walking the complete length of the stall-lined street, and I was fascinated as I watched the never-ending supply of people enjoy their sports of eating, bargaining, and gaming. As we left the stall area, Lodge hailed a taxi. It was now after ten o'clock, and I was surprised to find so many people yet out on the streets. As we drove along, Lodge asked, "Would you like to continue looking at some more homes tomorrow?" Perfectly happy with the house we'd found and made a gentleman's agreement on, I said, "No, thanks. I'm satisfied as long as you promise that Mr. Tze will have the house finished by August when I return with my family." "No problem," responded Lodge, "I'll keep a personal look after the progress."

After a brief lull in the conversation, I thought it might be well to ask, "Lodge, do you know of any land for sale near Fuchow, available for industrial construction? I'd like five to ten acres. I'm going out to look at the site we would have an option on in Nei Li, but I'd like something to compare to." "Would you mind if I go along with you?" he asked as our taxi pulled up in front of the hotel. "It would be my pleasure to have you along. What time would be convenient for you in the morning?" "Well," he said, "let's plan to get an early start. How about eight o'clock for breakfast?"

"Agreed," I said. Then, wanting to express my gratitude for the hospitality of both for a pleasant evening's enjoyment, I did my best in Western protocol, giving a firm but warm handshake, covering the two hand grasp with my other hand, saying in my best Chinese, "Hsieh Hsieh Nin, Hsieh Hsieh Nin." Both answered as they pulled away, Wan An, Mien Tien Jen."

The doorman smiled at me, as I watched them drive off, and said to me in his broken English, "Must be number one good friend. Wish you peaceful evening until tomorrow . . . a sign of true friendship." "You know, I have the same feeling for them," I said to him, giving him a coin RMB$5 tip for his courtesy, and I returned to my room with a warm, all the way through feeling of satisfaction, thinking, "These people are great."

Chapter 14

Looking for a Factory Site and School for the Kids Followed By a Treasure Hunt

It was eight o'clock sharp when I stepped out of the elevator to "Dzao, Tai Le Hsien Sheng" greetings of the starter and several of the desk clerks, including my favorite, Patty Chen.

As I walked toward the lobby doors, I spotted Lodge entering the hotel, a warm friendly smile on his face, extending his hand and saying, "Good morning, Tai Le. How are you on this fine Saturday morning? It's a beautiful day for a ride out into the country." Changing the subject with ease, he asked, "Ever had a Chinese breakfast before? Would you like to try it?"

"Whoa," I said, "you're about three questions ahead of my answers. First off, I'd like to say thanks for the enjoyable evening. I thoroughly enjoyed the better half of your family, and you make a fairly good host, too. Now, let me say 'Dzao' and answer your invitation to try a Chinese breakfast with a positive 'hao.' You know me, I'm game to try anything once."

"Good," he said, as we proceeded out to catch a taxi. "I know an excellent spot right downtown, and it's on our way to Nei Li."

The trip to the restaurant went quicker than I thought. Traffic was heavy but seemed to flow in a much more orderly manner than during the later parts of the day. "Lodge," I asked, "with the thousands of shops that line both sides of your boulevards, side streets, and small back alleys, ranging from VD clinics to banks, how do so many merchants survive in your economy? Do you have a lot of business failures?" Lodge replied, "That is one of the secrets of the Chinese. The business acumen of the Chinese merchant is legendary. We are a people who have specialized for centuries in retail trading, not only in our own country, but worldwide. The economies of many other countries in Southeast Asia are almost virtually dependent on the Chinese 'alien' community. The 'secret' involves many variables, like willingness to commit oneself to long hours, hard work, smart buying, and as you know from last night's purchase, they drive a hard bargain. Another secret is the loyalty and commitment of the 'family' to the business. Many of our retail businesses although small are vertically integrated, as you define it in your giant corporate terminology. The goods are often produced or raised in the home or on the farms of family members, sold direct to the retail outlet, thereby eliminating the 'wholesale' step in your distribution system. The success of a business is not measured on the basis of profitability per se, but on the strength of the business's ability to provide a comfortable living for the entire family. How well the family eats and is clothed and the fact that the elders can be taken care of . . . these are the important measuring sticks. The 'family' unit generally works very well together. Although age is usually a privileged factor within the family structure, when it comes to doing business, those members with native intelligence for business generally get the nod to lead and plan the business future."

Just as we were concluding our conversation, Lodge directed the taxi driver to pull over. As I got out of the car, I seemed to notice a certain degree of familiarity in my surroundings, and then as I spotted the Flower Club, I knew that we were near the Tai Fong Bank branch that would shortly become the site of my new offices.

Lodge turned and walked down the block several doors, and I followed him into a small, open front restaurant with no more than four tables, each about the size of a school desk. He spoke to one of the cooks in Chinese and then began to explain the forthcoming breakfast adventure. "A Chinese breakfast is usually not a fancy one. It consists of a large bowl of soupy rice, with some side dishes of pickles, somewhat like your relish, some coconut and raisins, a few pieces of dried beef or pork jerky. If you are really hungry, then you can have the equivalent of your breakfast rolls and doughnuts. See the man over there cooking at the barrel? He's making "sau bing," a slightly salted roll, covered with sesame seeds." "Like the roll that is served with the Mongolian barbeque?" I asked. "Exactly," was his answer, "and the other fellow is making a yeast dough doughnut stick, almost like a French doughnut. The doughnut is called 'yu tiao,' and most Chinese buy the two together. The 'yu tiao' is placed inside the 'sau bing' roll."

As the cook set two bowls of soupy rice in front of us and then one set of side dishes, I said to Lodge, "I'd really like to try the 'Sau bing yu tiao.'" "Do you know how to ask for one, in Chinese?" he asked. "No, but I'd like to learn," I replied. "I think that's going to be a great place to eat before going to work. You know why, our offices would be in the Tai Fong bank building right around the corner." "Sounds like a convenient set up. Although this restaurant isn't much on looks, I'm told they have the best 'sau bing yu tiao' in China." "OK," he began, "lesson number 1. 'Wau' means 'I' in English. 'Yau' is our word for want. So, you can order by simply saying, 'Wau yau sau bing yu tiao.' Try it."

A bit hesitant in speaking up, my first "Hsien Sheng" was not heard. Speaking again, I asked, "Hsien Sheng." When I had caught his attention, I ordered, "Ching, Wau yau sau bing yu tiao." I recognized his answer, "Hao le," but didn't understand his following question, "Dwo shao?" Looking at Lodge, I found him smiling . . . recognizing my predicament. Then, he said, "He wants to know how many you want." Immediately, I turned to the cook who was waiting for an answer and showed him one finger, which he acknowledged. Turning around at the sound of Lodge's voice, he was saying, "Guess I didn't take my teaching far enough," so we began to learn the numbers. Lodge took a napkin and said, "Write your numbers down, and then you can write the phonetic sound for the Chinese equivalent alongside it."

After writing it all down, I rehearsed, "Yee, er, san . . . hey, that's the same as three in Japanese . . . su, qu, liou, chi, ba jiou, shr." Now, said Lodge, "If you want to define how many pieces you want, just add a 'guh' to the number, so for your one piece order for 'sau bing yu tiao,' you'd say, 'yee guh.'" Just at that moment, the cook placed the extra order in front of me and said, "Yee guh sau bing yu tiao."

We finished our breakfast, which cost us all of RMB$24 or US$3, and walked about two blocks to a train station to take an express train to Chung Li. We pulled away within seconds of getting on, and within minutes, the train was speeding along its way south into the countryside. Crossing the river, one could see out across the rice paddy countryside for miles to a point where a lofty range of mountains rose, majestically touching into a pure white layer of clouds. Everything was so green and lush. Lodge broke the silence, saying, "Beautiful, isn't it?" "Almost pastoral," was my answer. "Mountains are the dominant feature of the island. They cover about 85 percent of the land area, leaving only 15 percent of the balance as arable, but the land that is farmed is among the most productive in the world. Fortunate for us, we are almost self-sufficient for meats and vegetables and feed one of the world's most dense people to land ratios. The sea around us also abounds with seafood, which you know are a staple to our diet. About the only commodity that we don't have enough of is the dairy products area. We have to import most of our dried milk and butter, but the government is experimenting with the build-up of a dairy herd to eventually produce our own."

Within twenty-five minutes, we had covered the twenty-five miles to Chung Li, and we got off there, the first stop on the train's way to the southernmost seaport which was another five hours ride.

Lodge and I navigated our way out of the crowded station, and he hailed a taxi. Before he would let me get in, he said, "Let me negotiate a fare for our way back, with this 'wild chicken.'" After he and the driver agreed on an RMB$50, US$6, we climbed in, and the driver took off down the road like a "chicken with its head off." Laughingly, I said, "Now I know how they got their label." Lodge agreed, but promised, "I'll try to slow him down so we get back alive."

Within five minutes, we were at the proposed plant site, which was in the Nei Li Industrial Park, the site of a former rice field. The streets had all been laid out, so it was easy to survey the plot of ground where ABC had taken an option on six thousand pings, about equivalent to five acres.

"How much will you have to pay per ping?" was Lodge's question. "The government has quoted roughly US$13,500 per acre," I answered. "Good price!" he stated. "Land right in or around Taipei will cost upwards of US$90,000-120,000. None of what I will show you will have the access to Highway 1 or the utilities like this site have. In fact, if we find land in some of these other areas, we'll probably have to negotiate with five or more landowners to get one single tract large enough for your needs. Frankly, although this site is about one and half hours from the city, by car, I think you'll find the labor market for factory workers will be better here, rather than in the city, where I feel there is a real shortage."

I had to take a complete walk around the property, stepping off the boundary lines . . . kind of like a King surveying his domain. I could kind of visualize the final plan in my mind, as to where the building should be located, the access, and exit traffic plans. Satisfied that I had a good feel for the lay of the land, we climbed back into the taxi and pointed ourselves back to the city.

Before we could turn around, I caught a glimpse of the Zenith, Bendix, Adams Gum, and DuPont buildings already in the park. "Now, these plants look as good, aesthetically and functionally, as any in the States," I told Lodge. As we headed back along Highway 1, I was impressed with the huge RCA, Timex, and Ampex plants, each of which had a different, but definite architectural appeal.

Shortly, our cab driver slowed down from his ninety kilometers per hour speed craze (only fifty miles per hour to a more moderate forty kilometers per hour) coming down the steep mountain road. By the time we had navigated our way through the mountain pass and snaked our way up and down the many curves in the mountain road. As we navigated our way back into the river places, I noticed that over one and a half hours had passed. "Lodge," I asked, "my boss told me when we were talking about this assignment that the travel time wouldn't be a problem . . . that an interstate highway with limited access was to be built and completed within the next few months." Lodge chuckled. "Yes, it's true that the government is building such a road and had promised to have it completed by 1971, but then again they had promised 1969, 1970, and 1971 in each successive year. My guess is that it will be complete by 1975." Pausing to let the impact of his humor sink in, he said, "Ever think of letting me find you a place out in Chung Li?" Each time we passed a hotel on the road, Lodge would point it out and say, "Now there's a nice hotel with hot and cold maids that you might be interested in considering." "Your humor isn't really funny," I said and we both laughed.

We looked at three other potential factory sites on our way back, one in Tao Yuan, another in Hsin Chuang, and the last in Sanchung city. All of them were really out of the way on very poor secondary roads. "Lodge, I guess I'll have to accept your evaluation and recommendations, even though the Nei Li site is presently inconvenient. When and if they do finish the highway, it will be the best site." "One other consideration," my realtor mentioned, "there are also plans on the drawing boards to locate our new international airport near Taoyuan, near the new highway, and it will be within ten minutes of your site." "No contest," was my conclusion. "ABC has just had its mind made up."

"Looks like we're almost home!" Lodge exclaimed, as we headed back into the city. "What are your plans for now?" "Well," I stated, "I thought I'd like to take the opportunity to visit the National Palace Museum this afternoon." "Great, I'm sure you'll enjoy the experience. It has some of China's greatest treasures. I'd like to accompany you, but I've promised to take another customer on a house-hunting tour, so if you'll excuse me, I'll plan to drop you off there. It's on my way home."

As we crossed over the bridge back into the city, our conversation gravitated toward the personal side, both of us exploring to learn more about each other's family. "Lodge, one of the projects I have to accomplish before I leave next Tuesday for home is to take a look at the International School, for my children." "Well," Lodge replied, "that's going to be right on our way to the Palace museum, so let's stop and take a look, OK?" Within two minutes, we were getting out of the cab to look over the school campus.

The International School facilities were a pleasant surprise. "Fantastic, I'm impressed with what I see," was my initial comment. "What do you know about the school?" I asked. "My knowledge is limited to what I hear from my customers and a few Chinese friends who work here. There are three separate school units, each with their own separate facilities. The elementary school with grades kindergarten through sixth is over here, the middle school for grades seven through nine is on our right, and the high school through twelfth grade is over beyond these middle school buildings. I understand they have about two thousand and five hundred students, and from what I hear, the educational concepts are very advanced." "Got a few minutes, Lodge, for me to get my camera out of the taxi and take some pictures? I know my kids will be pleased to see that they're going to be going to a first-class school . . . at least in terms of the facilities." Lodge picked up the conversation, as I returned and started taking pictures, saying, "Chinese educators would give up 'all the Tea in China' for a setup like this."

We continued to walk and explore to find an auditorium, separate gymnasium, a fully equipped cafeteria, and a complete athletic field setup for football, baseball, soccer, and tennis. "Looks like they've got everything, doesn't it?" I remarked. "Yes, but many Chinese people, merchants around the school, and taxi drivers complain about the unruliness, lack of manners, and the slovenly look of dress of many of the students. They feel the school officials and the parents are far too permissive in regulating and disciplining the children's behavior." "Lodge, I know exactly what you are referring to. They are a product of the 'ugly American' abroad, that one hears so much about. They really aren't typical of what most 'Americans' are like back home." "One of the major problems that concerns the Chinese in our community is the extent of the drug problem amongst the American and International teenagers. So many have seen the tragic effects of opium among our own, many years ago, and they fear that the foreigners are going to develop a similar social tragedy in the near future." "How did Chinese solve the opium problem?" I queried. "Very simple," he replied, "the use of opium and heroin was limited by law to usage only by those with terminal diseases, to ease their suffering. The penalty of execution on the spot was applied to those caught selling or using drugs without the medical need. That type of 'dictatorial' action has stopped the problem from becoming a cancer of our society." "Very effective, I'm sure," was my only reaction.

Satisfied with our tour of the International School, we hopped back into the taxi and took off for the Palace Museum. As we passed the VW showroom and then turned down a small side street, I began to recognize the familiar surroundings, the small shops, and then the rice fields and gardens. Lodge asked, "Know where we're at?" It dawned on me then that the school was going to be within five to ten minutes driving time from our new home. "Lodge," I remarked, "sure looks like you've picked out the RIGHT house for us . . . pardon the pun . . . convenient to school and the shops of Tien Mou, but yet out and away from the rest of the world. Hsieh Hsieh Ni."

Within five minutes, the cab was pulling up in front of another impressive structure of Chinese architecture, very picturesquely nestled into the verdant mountain hillside . . . the National Palace Museum. Lodge said, "Bob, I'd really like to go with you. I enjoy wandering through this house of art treasures. They help me appreciate my ancestry and China's place in development of man's cultural endeavors. It serves to give one a sense of pride in belonging to the Chinese race." Pausing, he suggested, "Take one of the English-speaking tours that start every hour on the hour. Then after you've made the rounds once, you may want to go back to look at some of the items a second time." "Gee," I remarked looking at my watch, "if I hustle, I can probably catch the two o'clock tour. Call me at the hotel on Monday, Lodge, so we can wrap up the details of our house rental agreement with Mr. Tze," I said as I paid the taxi driver and then said, "Dzai Jen, dzai Jen" and then began the long climb up the stairs through the multicolumned arch to the Palace.

Each step up the long stairway to the museum gave one a real spiritual lift. I felt myself coming closer to the real clues and initial first-hand introduction to the wonders of Chinese culture, a history of over five thousand years of civilization. Pausing to look and take pictures of the beautiful palace structure, built as recently as 1965, I marveled that the Chinese had retained their craftsmanship abilities to recreate the treasures of the past. It was a perfect blend of classical architecture of the Chou Dynasty of almost thousand years B.C. The four-story main building was adjoined by two outrigger wings built of light yellow bricks inlaid with quartz, with a roof of glazed green tiles.

I paid the entrance fee of RMB$20, about US$2.50, and after checking/leaving my camera (no picture taking is allowed), I joined the tour group of twenty which left for an hour's walk through the three exhibition rooms, four galleries, and two halls especially for sculptures. Our very pretty, and scholarly, lady tour guide explained, "The museum was built in 1965 specifically to show the rest of the world the 600,000 pieces of art spanning thirty centuries of history. It is dedicated to Dr. Sun Yat-sen, the founder of the Republic of China." She continued, "Approximately 3,000 pieces of the collection are shown, with many of the objects being rotated each three months. The art treasures include some of the finest and most well-preserved bronze vessels, porcelain china, lacquer wares, carved ivory and jade, many tapestries, silk brocades, and scroll paintings, representing each of the forty-nine Imperial family periods dating back to 2205 BC."

The tour was much too fast to really fully appreciate the significance of the things I was seeing. Of particular interest to me were the Oracles of China, almost four thousand years old. These were the first evidences of their written language and had been carved into the soft bone undershell of huge land tortoises. The porcelain pieces traced the first known relationship between the Eastern and Western cultures. It is believed that the beautiful cobalt blues used as dyes in their porcelain were imported from Persia. This belief is well founded, when one observes many Islamic decorative motifs in these products of the Yuan dynasty of the thirteenth and fourteenth centuries AD. The genius of the Chinese is evidenced in the many rare books and writings in their collection of over 150,000 some of which were printed some two hundred years before the Gutenberg Bible.

I left the museum at closing time, 5:00 p.m., with the feeling of being an insignificant speck in the history of man, yet with a definite desire to return to this magnificent storehouse of historical treasures.

As I rode home toward the hotel, I was totally oblivious to the suicidal tendencies of my taxi driver and all of the activities of the present-day world. It was obvious to me, however, that I would thoroughly enjoy my exploration into Chinese history and culture and that I had much to learn from these people who were the foundation to our modern-day world civilizations.

Chapter 15

More Cultural Exposure

Still somewhere up on that 'cloud nine' thinking of my earlier cultural exposure at the museum, I really didn't appreciate the forthcoming nature of my full-fledged transition into the art of Chinese social enjoyment, in the same classical sense, until I realized that I was standing in the lobby of the Hotel Sincere in the infamous locale of Peitou, as C. C. Chiu introduced me to his six business compatriots of the Tai Fong bank . . . our wine, women, and song warrior companions for the night.

In the proper pecking order, I shook hands with T. S. Chiang, the bank's chairman, then B. Y. Huang, the president, and Messrs. Wu and Lin of the Shanghai Road branch office, who had so warmly sponsored my membership to the "Flower Club," and finally, Messrs. Wei and Peng of the Chung Li branch. The surroundings and appointments of the hotel were first class. They gave one a very warm welcome and intimate feeling as the Madame escorted us to a private room. It dawned on me that although I'd never been here before, I felt as if I had been, and then remembered the article in a recent issue of the *Time* magazine describing in precise dimensions, all about the facilities and routine of the Hotel Sincere . . . almost made me feel like a celebrity to revisit such a famous institution. It left me with an overactive imagination of things to come.

Our room was large enough to accommodate two separate tables. One half of the room was done in Japanese fashion with tatami mat floor with a low 'chow' table and pillows to cater to the Japanese clientele. The other half provided a circular Chinese-style dining table plus a complete settee of furniture capable of accommodating at least eight persons. No sooner than we had entered the room, and followed the lead of Chairman Chiang in taking off our suit coats, then the drinks began to flow and the hors d'oeuvres, including eight obviously handpicked Chinese beauties, were brought in. Imagine to my surprise, as the introductions were being made, to see the one and same student teacher, upon whose lovely legs my eyes had feasted while on her motorbike perch reading a book, several days before on my way to Barry Frazier's house for cocktails. She was even more beautiful than I had remembered in my fleeting glance, not sexy beautiful, just wholesome beautiful.

Quickly, I nudged Cecil and whispered to him that I'd like to be paired up with my secretly admired courtesan, which he relayed to Chairman Chiang who quickly obliged. When it came time to introduce me to Mei Ling, all of a sudden, I became the center of attraction to the other blushing and snickering girls. An American in their midst was not an everyday occurrence. Mei Ling stood out as something very special; just the way she moved and walked, one could tell she had poise, an air of confidence, but yet as she walked toward me, she radiated a humbleness in her charms. I thought to myself as I watched her, "What will be the outcome of this match between expert and novice in this art of entertaining and being entertained?" With ease, she did a very convincing job of making me, in my naive manner, feel exactly as she designed. I was to be the 'King for a Night,' and my every wish was to be her every command. Feeling a little uncomfortable, kind of like the 'fly in the spider's web,' I wondered if my twinge of anxiety was apparent.

Mei Ling was dressed in an exquisite Chinese 'chi pou' dress of red silk brocade, the fit of which served to accentuate her very pleasing shape. She was taller than the average Chinese girl, probably 5'5" inches with long legs and well-proportioned hips and breasts. Her skin of honey-color appeared smooth and soft. She wore little or no makeup. A beautiful smile radiated from her face, and she took my hands, looked up at me, and spoke in her soft, kitten-like voice, "Tai Le Hsien Sheng, I am Mei Ling." Leading me by the hand, we proceeded to navigate our way to a corner settee, where we both sat down. Not knowing where to start the conversation, I waited for her to take the initiative. She, cautious of her English, hesitated for a few moments, but what seemed like an hour. We just sat and looked at each other. It became apparent for both that our words tonight would be few, but as both of us responded to each other, I could feel the chemistry working, drawing us closer together. "Who was it," I thought, "that said, 'A picture is worth a thousand words.'" It must have been Confucius.

As we both enjoyed the guarded chemical relationship, she began to move quietly to make sure that I had something to drink and a few hors d'oeuvres to nibble on. Each time she broke the contact of our togetherness, I had a chance to look on and listen to the rest of the group. They had paired off, each with a female companion, and had seated themselves, eight of them at the round table and the rest at the 'chow' table. Judging from the noise, the hand games and the drinking activity, all were having a great time.

Words between us began to flow as our feelings for each other developed, but not without difficulty. Mei Ling set the tone of our conversation, saying, "You not like other Wei Kuo Ren, Foreigner, I think in English. You feeling for me is more than physical. I am happy! May I stay with you all night?" I didn't quite know how I was going to answer that question and not wanting to make any irrevocable commitments, my discretion became the better part of my desire, so I began to explain, slowly, "Mei Ling, I want very much to spend the evening with you." She smiled her understanding. "How old are you?" I asked. "Twenty," she said, her smile continuing. Stumped for more words, I was thankful when our awkward situation was interrupted by Chairman Chiang and C.C. The Chairman spoke with a glow on his face, with comments directed at both Mei Ling and myself, while C.C.

interpreted, saying, "Chairman Chiang is happy to see that both of you are indeed enjoying each other's company, and Tai Le, he would like to compliment you for your taste in women. Your pick of Mei Ling has been indeed a sacrifice for him. Mei Ling is one of his most favorite women, and the fact that you are obviously well matched is a source of some small frustration for he had looked forward to her favor for this evening." Feeling very guilty of depriving the chairman of his pleasure, I attempted to offer to switch my attentions but was quickly interrupted by Cecil who cautioned, "Do not be hurt if I ignore your suggestion, which would make three persons unhappy this evening. Chairman Chiang would lose face to everyone if you were to direct your attentions to another. Mei Ling would also lose face, for she truly likes you as a person, more like a Chinese than foreigner, and finally, you, too, would feel bad, for the others are not in the same class as Mei Ling. So, Chairman Chiang, as a gentleman, would hope that you enjoy your evening with Mei Ling. Now, let's eat. Would you enjoy Chinese style or Japanese sukiyaki?" "C.C.," I responded, "as an old Western philosopher once said, 'When in Rome, do as the Romans do,' so I'd prefer Chinese food." Taking Mei Ling by the hand and following C.C., we all sat down, Mei Ling between Chairman Chiang and myself.

Chairman Chiang opened the festivities with gusto, offering Shiao Shing wine and Pi Jyou beer in a series of "gam bei" toasts to welcome me, then the companionship, then the pleasures of the Hotel, and finally, with many red faces, not from embarrassment but from drinking, to the meal. The meal wasn't all that great, and C.C., sensing that the cuisine wasn't the feature attraction, jokingly commented to the humor of all that, "Although the food doesn't begin to compare with that of the Grand Hotel, the deliciousness of this meal the Grand Hotel can't match . . . the girls."

The more alcohol flowed, the more the games became a part of our diet, and the noise level increased. The hand came of matching fingers with shouted numbers began amongst the men at the "chow" table. The loser of each contest was obliged to "gam bei," a glass of rice wine, the girls doing their duty each time to refill the glass. In a space of five minutes, it was obvious that one could get a good start on a roaring drunk if you lost too frequently. Mei Ling explained, as we watched Mr. Lin, the assistant manager of Shanghai Road branch, getting the best of Mr. Wei, his peer from the Ching Li branch. Out of loyalty to her man, Tuan Tuan began to drink for him. Tuan Tuan's part seemed only to heighten Lin's desire to drink Wei under the table, so she became the object of the challenge match, her favors to the winner. Actually, I knew that the loser wasn't going to be able to do any favors.

Another hand game, that of kindergarten level, rock paper scissors, started between some of the men at our table. The consequence of this game was the same. Mei Ling teasingly taught me how to play, and before I knew it, I was in a contest with Chairman Chiang.

It was obvious, after I had been forced into several "gam bei's," that I was matching wits with an expert. However, with some fine coaching from Mei Ling, I was able to hold my own for about ten rounds. After which, however, I was reeling a little bit like we were boxing, when all of a sudden I was saved from a TKO by a ruckus across the room which caught everyone's attention. Mr. Lin had won Tuan Tuan from Mr. Wei, and they were having a playful exchange of words. He was refusing her favors, claiming she was not a virgin and espousing that the victorious warrior was entitled to one.

Chairman Chiang interrupted the melee of words, with an admonishment to conduct themselves in good faith. C.C. translated the story, as Chiang lectured, in all modesty about the three brothers who married on the same night. On the next day, they began to compare notes on the disappointments of their wedding night, when they all found out that their new brides and families had deceived them. Each found his betrothed to be more experienced than advertised. Of course, they had been led into believing that they were taking virgins for their wives.

All three complained simultaneously to the village matchmaker, who told them philosophically, "Even if your brides had been virgins last night, they would not be so today. After all, you do not sleep with a good woman just for a single night, do you?" Spontaneous laughter erupted from the entire group. As it subsided, Mr. Lin took Tuan Tuan by the hand, who resisted, taunting him with a question, to which another gut-ache type of laughter exploded. Cecil translated as the two disappeared. "She's telling Lin now that he knows that she was a virgin once, she wants to know if he is an egg?" Mei Ling blushed and hung her head, obviously embarrassed at knowing the story behind that question.

C.C. hedged on the full translation, saying, "I'd better tell you that one when we're alone, another time." One by one, it was obvious that several of the couples had slipped away for other sporting events, while others had chosen to play Mahjong. Now ten o'clock and sensing my earlier timidity about a physical relationship, hoping to build my ego image, or at least not wanting to feel embarrassed as the last couple remaining, which would have exposed a scene of frigidity between us to the others, Mei Ling took my hand and beckoned for me to follow. As we arose, Chairman Chiang took us both by the hand and told us a story, in Chinese. C.C. was not around to translate, so I watched their facial expressions intently. He was enjoying himself as he talked. Mei Ling's face took on an expression of sincerity, yet with a radiant glow. She was an exquisite person. When he had finished, she squeezed my hand and whispered, "I will tell you the story, later tonight." Then, with a warm handshake from Chairman Chiang, we took leave from him. She spoke quietly, "Chiang Hsien Sheng say to me, tell you goodnight. He leave for home, soon. He will await your call Monday, on business matters."

As we walked down the stairs to a ground-level area, the air became thick and moist. I sensed immediately that we were leading up to what Peitou was famous for, the ritual of the bath, a social custom of centuries in the Orient, one that I had thoroughly enjoyed during my residency in Japan some ten years prior. I wondered if the ceremony here would be similar. We entered our own cubicle, each of us to enjoy the privacy of a separate dressing room. A bamboo wicker basket was provided for one's clothes. A small stool was the only other utility provided, save for the white cotton kimono-type robe and towel. I put the towel around my waist before donning the robe and wandering from my enclosure out into the bathing area. The bath house gave me the feeling of being in a hospital. It appeared so sterile. The walls and pool were done in white ceramic tile offset only with borders of blue tile trim. The bath water was hot, with clouds of steam puffing up from the surface of the pool, which was about 3' by 5' and about 3-1/2' deep. I stood waiting until Mei Ling came out from her side. Her kimono differed from mine, only in that it was adorned with blue chrysanthemum flowers. Although it did not reveal her lovely figure as well as her "chi pou," the outline of her body shown through as a silhouette in the shadows of the light. She moved very quietly and efficiently to get me maneuvered onto a small stool and then helped me take off my robe. Giggling, as she saw my towel modesty, she said, "You like Japanese men." "Yes," I replied, "I enjoyed many baths in Japan where I lived." First, she started to massage my neck and back, her expert hands relaxing my tense muscles almost immediately. As she gradually proceeded to massage my arms, chest, and legs, facing me, I felt fortunate that I had gone through this experience before and had learned to exercise mind over matter in control of the most embarrassing muscles on the male body. Thoroughly relaxing me, she proceeded to soap my body and then rinse me off with water that was pleasantly warm. As she washed, she proceeded to relate the essence of the fatherly story told by Chairman Chiang prior to our leaving.

Shyly, she said, "Ni yun-lin, a painter from many centuries ago, insisted on cleanliness very much. One night, after a great feast, he took a famous woman. She bathed with him, but he was not satisfied, so they bathed many times. Finally, when they were ready to enjoy each other, he found out that it was morning, too late because he had very important appointment with government official. So he had to leave her. Chairman Chiang advised me to make sure you not miss tenderness of tonight before important meeting on your schedule tomorrow morning."

Finishing the story, she took my hand and placed the soap in my palm. It probably was a godsend that I wasn't expected to be her masseuse, as I'm not sure that the same mind would have had the same control, if I had been expected to massage her body. So, after removing her robe, I restricted my activities to soaping and rinsing her neck, back, and arms. Sensing my awkwardness, she took over to ready herself for the piece de resistance, the soaking bath.

After rinsing her body, Mei Ling was into the tub watching me gingerly test the water with my foot. Accustomed to the almost boiling point of the pool water, she laughed as I proceeded to plunge in, ankle-deep, then out again, and then into the water up to the knee cap. It must have taken at least five minutes before I was capable of withstanding the heat up to my neck. The next thirty minutes were spent in pure physical ecstasy as we sat there, facing each other, sitting on a small ledge built into over two sides of the pool, our bodies soaking up the bath's mesmeric as well as it's therapeutic value. Neither of us dared to touch each other and destroy the cleanliness and purity that comes to one's mind . . . exactly as it was intended. One thought that kept coursing through my mind that disturbed my tranquility, would my wife understand the innocence of this situation, as I kept remembering the divorce outcome of the *Time* magazine article that showed the Marine Lieutenant enjoying his bath with his tub mate. I prayed that the sanctuary of this bath would not be invaded by the candid camera.

Beet red, looking like a lobster, and feeling like a wet noodle, Mei Ling helped me on with my robe. She rinsed the bathroom down with several buckets of scalding hot water, and I picked up my basket of clothes. From the bath, we entered a steam room off the bath where she motioned for me to lie down on a massage table built close to the floor, low enough so she could kneel at the side and perform the gentle art of massaging and soothing one's body into a total state of relaxation. As she kneaded my muscles with her strong hands and fingers, she whispered, "I not usually do this, but I want to do, for you." Then she explained, slowly, that the massage was normally done by blind persons. She said,

"My government build special schools, to train blind people to do this work. They really good, maybe you like to try?" At this point in time, enjoying my relationship with her, I said, "Not this time, Mei Ling. I don't want to break the spell of happiness that you have created." Pleased, she continued taking special care not to hurt my tender muscles.

When we finished, we left the bath area, still in our robes, and walked up several flights of stairs to a group of rooms, all accessible, Japanese-style, through sliding "shoji" rice paper doors. We sat at a small "chow" table on the tatami mat floor. Mei Ling poured each of us a cup of hot tea that was on the table. The tea had a very pleasant aroma, a scent of flowers. Quietly, she told me, "This tea made with blossom of jasmine." Somehow, it put the right touch on the tenderness of this whole evening.

After taking just a few sips of her tea, she moved around the table and gently took my hand, leading me to a spot where we lie down, side by side, resting our heads on a small stuffed pillow. Minutes went by as we both enjoyed our moments of reverie. Slowly and gently, I realized she was turning on her side, pressing her lithe body against mine and then laying her head on my chest. "Tai Le Hsien Sheng," she said softly, "now you feel like my father or older brother?"

My mind started racing for an answer. How does one say no to an obvious offer of physical pleasure, but then how would I live with the conscience of guilt with my wife? How does one answer "Yes" without hurting the obvious pride she has taken in pleasing me? For a moment, I question the validity of the moral ethic of our Western religious codes regarding "adultery" and "thy neighbor's wife," but answer, I must.

Looking at her in the eyes, I decide to be honest and direct. "Mei Ling, I do not feel like your father or your brother. My feelings for you are as a man. You are a lovely woman whom any man would find easy to love. 'Love' to me is not just a physical attraction. It is the match of a man and woman, of their minds, spirits, feelings, and a physical union. Sex for sex sake is not love." Pausing to watch her reaction, I was pleased to know she understood. She nodded and waited for me to continue.

"A man can, honestly, love only one woman. Any others in his life, other than his wife, mother, or daughters, are purely for the object of a sex relationship, excluding, of course, those regarded in the relationship of a friend." Pausing again to find her face radiating understanding, I took her hand and said, "Mei Ling, if I were not married, I'm sure as we got to know each other, I feel we could find 'love' for each other. I'm sure we could also find friendship, but already I know I respect you as a person too much to enjoy a relationship anytime, purely for sex."

The look on her face was magnificent. A slight smile parted her lovely lips and her eyes glistened with agreement. She said, "Tai Le Hsien Sheng, your words sound like those of Chinese philosophy. We think the same about love, friends, and sex. Do not feel me unhappy. I am pleased. In the future, we will truly enjoy a togetherness as friends."

Upon her note of open invitation, we both got up and left the room. "Wait for me," I said as I hurried to get myself dressed. During her absence, I couldn't help but think of the sensitiveness of the evening. Searching for a word to describe Mei Ling as a person was difficult, but when the word "delicate" came to mind, I was satisfied. Within minutes, she was back. Then taking my hands in hers, she looked up at me and said, "Wau ai ni. (It means I love you.) Even if you cannot say to me, I can . . . to you." Without another word, she led me back to the party room where we had had our dinner. As she opened the door, I could see C.C. sitting in a chair fast asleep. He was waiting for me to take me back to the hotel.

Although we said our "Hsieh Hsieh Ni's" and "Dzai Jen's" to each other, they were perfunctory. Our real feelings toward each other, as the evening's pleasure, had already been spoken much earlier. Moments later, C.C. and I were in a cab on our way back to the hotel. C.C. was anxious to know how I enjoyed the evening. Hoping to express my pleasure adequately, I chose to say "Ding hao." Obviously pleased, he responded, "Hen hao le," and then, as if bursting to speak on another subject, he began, "Now, as I promised, let me translate the *folktale* about Mr. Lin and the egg."

Not wanting to spoil the mood of the evening, I apologized to C.C. and asked if he could relate the tale some other day. With obvious sensitivity, so exquisitely practiced by the Chinese, he acknowledged his understanding, and we arrived at the hotel with the mood intact.

Footnote: *The Dragon and the Phoenix*; Eric Chou; 1971. Paraphrased from story on pages 253-254.

Ibid., pages 259-260.

CHAPTER 16

Sight Seeing First Class

Fortunately, I'd checked my mailbox after coming home from Peitou to find a note from Tien Lai advising me to be in the lobby at 8:15 in the morning and not to forget to bring my camera for our trip into the interior today.

Even with skipping breakfast to catch an extra hour's sleep, the night seemed all too short with only five hours sleep. "Maybe," I thought, "I could catch up with some extra shut-eye on the plane." But then looking out the window to see a beautiful, clear, blue-sky day blossom was an excellent stimulus to getting going.

Tien Lai was right on time, and within five minutes, we were at the airport going through the security check, which for a domestic flight surprised me as being more strict than any I'd ever gone through on international flights. "Why the security check?" I asked. His usual sparkling personality showed a slight reticence to answer but with a catch of humor, he replied, "We can't afford to have any planes hijacked. With all the tourist business, we haven't got enough to handle our domestic air business, let alone help any other countries." Rather than press the topic, I changed the subject. Soon, we were called to board. As we boarded our FAT flight, I gave up any thought of sleep as I recognized our bird was a DC-3. I wondered how many tries it had made "over the hump."

As we entered the cabin, Tien Lai in the lead, we were greeted by the stewardess, who I must say was one of the most beautiful women I had ever looked upon, Western, Oriental, or otherwise. Tien Lai apparently knew her as he spoke to her, in Chinese, and then he introduced me to Linda Sheng. In answer to her "Good morning, Mr. Tai Le. Welcome to our flight," I mustered a weak "Dzao, ni hao ma?" Pleased with my attempt at Chinese, she smiled and complimented me obviously out of courtesy, "Very good." Realizing that we were holding up the rest of the passengers from boarding, she volunteered to continue the conversation, saying, "May I speak with you later, after we are airborne?"

As we took our seats, I asked, "Tien Lai, thanks for the introduction. You've helped take my mind off my need to sleep and my fear of DC-3's. You mentioned Linda's last name was Sheng, same as yours. Any relation?" "Yes," he replied quite proudly. "She is my younger sister, an identical twin." "She is truly beautiful. I'd like to have the chance to meet her sister also. You know, I have an identical twin brother, and although we look alike, we are very different." "Yes, I remember you told Moon on your first night here, so I'd like you to meet the other twin, Jennifer. She is also a stewardess for CAL. You will meet her on the way back from Taroko Gorge, tonight."

By now, the plane was airborne, and we were flying over some of Asia's most rugged and majestic mountains. With hardly a cloud in the sky, it appeared as if one could almost look down the entire length of the island and see nothing but a continuous range of mountains that forms the spine of this lush and lovely island. Interrupting our view of this beautiful panorama was the sight of Linda, who was now offering us some tea and spring roll hors d'oeuvres. She initiated the conversation, again complimenting, "Mr. Tai Le, you speak Chinese very well. My brother has told me about you that you are also a twin. My sister and I are anxious to talk with you, to get to know you better. We want to learn if twins are also a 'double lucky' sign in your country for your family." "No," I said, laughingly, "twins in America are regarded only as 'double trouble.'" She reacted with a most pleasing laugh, at my humor, and then disappeared to serve the rest of the passengers.

"My two sisters have brought much happiness in our family," said Tien Lai. "Linda is now married to a pilot. They work only on same flights. Linda insists you know the many stories about pilots and stewardesses. Jennifer is now twenty-three, single, and my family wants to find a nice, respectable man for her. How about you, Tai Le Hsien Sheng?" I didn't know if his question was in jest or humor, but I thought I'd better play it straight and answered, "Tien Lai, you know I am already married and the father of three teenage children." He smiled and laughed lightly. "You know my family would be honored to have you take Jennifer as a No. 2 wife. I'll speak with your wife to ask her permission, hao bu hao?" Then we both broke out in a hearty laugh.

I caught a brief glimpse of the east coast of the China. The mountains appeared to rise right out of the sea straight up to their peaks, making this area only accessible by air or sea. "Where is the East Coast highway?" I inquired. As the pilot began to take the plane into its landing approach, into a small sea coast port about mid-island, Tien Lai pointed out, "You see the line halfway up the mountain? That is the road. We must try it one time when your family comes. It is a once in a lifetime experience." About that time, we were on the ground, and as we exited the plane, Tien Lai stopped to talk with Linda, in Chinese. I said my "Dzai Jens" and told her, "I sure enjoyed meeting you and look forward to seeing your 'double.'" To which she replied, "We will, I promise."

Once we were inside the airport, Tien Lai was besieged with drivers wanting to take us up for the trip through the Gorge, and in true Chinese spirit, Tien Lai was negotiating the best price. For a change and comfort, he arranged for a Toyota Crown sedan for a most reasonable RMB$100. The equivalent of US$12 a day, gas and driver included, wouldn't even get you the keys to a Hertz car in the States. We drove about fifteen minutes along the coast, and then the entrance to Taroko Gorge appeared as we passed through a gate, along a swift, rugged boulder-choked stream emptying from the mountains into the sea. As we entered this canyon, one began to feel rather insignificant in the shadow of nature, its walls of marble towering hundreds of feet above the narrow, winding road. "This road was built about fifteen years before and it is our cross country highway. Over ten thousand men worked for four years. Many men died," explained Tien Lai, as we passed the Eternal Spring shrine, a memorial to 450 men who died in the process of building this engineering feat. At many places in the road, the sheer cliffs of marble were so close together one had to look up to see the sky, and the sun rarely reached the bottom, except at midday. In those areas, wide enough to look around, the multicolors of the exposed marble and granite looked like an abstract work of art. The marble stone from the riverbed up to road level had a smooth, glistening surface of marbled white and black having been polished for centuries by the raging waters. The walls above graduated from rough rock to the ever lush greens of this tropical paradise.

Along the road, we saw a few native aborigines of the Ami tribe. "Handsome people, except for their facial tattoos," I commented. "The Ami, they came from the South Pacific many hundreds of years ago," explained Tien Lai. "They are the same family of people as your Hawaiians." Their colorful red, turquoise, yellow, and white costumes somewhat resembled the dress of our Navajo Indians.

We navigated our way slowly past the Grotto of Swallows where many birds nest in the rocky crevices and caves and then through another especially winding, tunneled area appropriately called the Tunnel of Nine Turns, over a splendid marble banistered bridge guarded by two magnificent temple lions of alabaster at each end, spanning a rugged river adorned with many beautiful cataracts of water and dotted with smooth and oddly shaped boulders.

I counted a total of fifty-one tunnels as we came to the end of this spectacular ride over the twelve-mile road that found us about one and half hours later at the Tien Hsiang Lodge.

The lodge looked like a classical "Shangri La" nestled in this valley of nature's true wonders. "Here, we should have lunch, after which we can spend some time with Buddha in his temple, you see, in the hills over the Lodge. About 2:30 we must go back to Hualien." I remarked, as we walked around and looked at the beautiful landscaped grounds, the gardens, and swimming pool, "This would be a great place for a honeymoon." "Or a secret love affair," Tien Lai replied with a twinkle in his eye.

After another of the typical Chinese light lunches of six courses, amply supplemented with the one and only rice beer, "pei jyou," we crossed a suspension bridge over the Ri Yu river and climbed the stairs to the site of the temple and my first chance to see an authentic pagoda. Tien Lai took me into the temple, lavishly decorated in traditional Chinese red lacquer. The altar and many of the accessories to the worship service were trimmed in gold. One of the monks explained that this temple contained many art treasures dating back to the Sung dynasty, a thousand years ago. The temple had a very fragrant essence which Tien Lai explained, "The smell of blossoms is from incense." We watched for a brief moment, as several persons lit their incense sticks and placed them at the altar and then committed themselves to prayer. Then they moved to an adjacent altar and with the help of the monk, cast two oddly shaped wooden blocks on the floor. Tien Lai whispered, as we watched the monk take a cup and place some wood pieces into it, "Now he will shake the pieces in the cup and roll them out on the floor. The pieces will then reveal some thoughts of wisdom or saying of fortune for the day. Would you like to try?" "Sure," I said, "but only if it would not be considered sacrilegious for a non-Buddhist." He responded; "Anyone, religious or not, can try." So, Tien Lai asked the monk to tell my fortune. After I dropped the blocks and he rolled the cup, he gave my fortune, in Chinese characters on a paper, to Tien Lai, who philosophized, "In a man's mind, the best grain belongs to the other farmer. The prettiest woman is always the other man's wife." "Interesting," I said, "to see the similarity between the Oriental philosophy and our own Western belief that 'the grass is always greener on the other side of the fence.'"

Leaving a RMB$10 coin in the collection box for our newfound wisdom, Tien Lai and I left the temple to explore the pagoda. He explained, "Our pagoda was made to store and lock the treasures of the temple from bandits." After climbing the seven sets of stairs in cork-screw fashion to the top with difficulty, for a bird's-eye view of the Lodge and the canyon, the trip down was a breeze. "It's always easier for fish to go downstream, than up," was Tien Lai's analogy.

The trip back to Hualien we made with leisure. "You know, Tien Lai, I think a person could spend many days in a place like this to seek peace of one's mind and spirit that so often become confused in our complex society of today's world." "Tai Le Hsien Sheng," he said, "sometimes you speak like you think like Chinese, so you will like China."

Back at the Hualien airport, to board our plane for the trip back home, I was pleased to see that we had graduated from the Flying Tiger DC-3 to the later vintage DC-4 of China Airlines, and more anxious to meet the second half of the Tseng twins, Jennifer. Tien Lai introduced me as we entered the cabin, and before we could speak, I wondered how it was possible to tell Jennifer from Linda, a problem my parents had had with my brother and me. Her warm smile was followed by a soft and very beguiling, "Good evening, Mr. Tai Le. I've been looking forward to meeting you, ever since my brother called me to say that you would be on my flight. Did you enjoy the tour of Taroko Gorge?" To which I responded, "It is one of the most beautiful and spectacular wonders of nature that I've seen, and I thoroughly enjoyed myself, thanks to your brother." Again, the pressure of other boarding passengers forced us to postpone our conversation till the plane was in the air. Soon after takeoff, Jennifer was serving some delicious meat and fish hors d'oeuvres and fresh orange juice. She cautioned, "Now don't eat too much and ruin your appetite for dinner at the Blue Skies Restaurant," and then I caught her wink to Tien Lai. Sensing that her signal had special significance, I pursued the clue. "What was the wink for?" But all I could get from Tien Lai was an acknowledgment of "Special surprise, special surprise." The flight was full, and Jennifer had her hands full taking care of all the passengers in the forty-minute flight, so our conversation was limited to departing remarks. "Mr. Tai Le," she said, invitingly, "I hope I will see you soon?" Questioning, how I should respond, I formally replied, showing off my limited Chinese with a "Hsieh Hsieh Ni and Dzai jen, Jennifer."

As our taxi dropped me off at the hotel at 6:10, Tien Lai asked, "Will 7:15 be too soon? If not, I will meet you here. Dress with sport coat . . . no tie . . . is OK, OK?" With a "hao le" answer, the taxi was fading into the oncoming sunset.

Chapter 17

For Dinner: East Meets West

Within five minutes after picking me up in the lobby of the President Hotel, Tien Lai and I were deposited by our taxi in front of the Chia Hsin building on Chung Shan North Road. The clean, modern architectural lines of this new twelve-story office building graced by the beauty of water fountains and gardens made me realize that China was indeed well advanced in its contemporary architectural community, as well as the world economic plan.

Within seconds after entering our elevator, we were whisked to the top floor and walked into the Blue Skies Restaurant, equal in its feeling of plushness and commanding view of this metropolitan city, with that of the "Top of the Mark" in San Francisco. Tien Lai took me on a tourists' tour around the three exposed sides to view the panorama. Now in transition from a day of sunshine and clear blue skies to an approaching evening, where the lights glimmer like jewels. The brilliant sun sank like a fireball over the horizon making the clouds glow in beautiful shades of fire red and then fade into the night. "Tien Lai," I remarked, "look over there to the southwest. You can still see the outline of the mountains and the white clouds that cover them almost look like our Niagara Falls."

"I agree, hen hao fun jing," was his answer. "I also have some beautiful scenery over here," he said as he redirected my attention to a table of people awaiting our arrival. I found myself somewhat flustered as seating arrangements were made. I had assumed that the two of us were going to enjoy a leisurely evening meal talking business, and suddenly, I found myself being seated not only next to but in between the lovely company of the twins, Jennifer and Linda. After an introduction to Linda's husband, Paul Lin, I began to regain a little composure but still found myself bordering on bashfulness.

Now it dawned on me as to what all the conversation had been about on the planes between Tien Lai and his sisters. "Tien Lai," I said, "I'm going to make a special effort to learn Chinese as soon as I return with my family so I can overhear and anticipate some of your future surprises."

"Why are you so nervous, Tai Le Hsien Sheng?" asked Linda. "Isn't this a pleasant surprise?" To which I responded, "It isn't the pleasant surprise that makes me nervous, but the fact that I'm sitting between two such beautiful women AND that I'm not prepared to entertain that makes me uncomfortable." Jennifer looked at me with confidence in her eyes and said in a soft, but reassuring voice, "Tai Le Hsien Sheng, don't you worry about entertaining us. We will take good care of you. I know how to make you happy. If you are happy, then I will be happy. Hao bu hao?"

With that, a feeling of assurance came over me, and I accepted the offer, saying, "Hao," but qualified my commitment by saying, "It's a good thing that Linda's husband Paul is here, because I know I couldn't handle two such gracious ladies, one of you is all that I'm going to be able to keep up with." I guess I said it right because Paul started to laugh and was followed by the others.

"Now, how would you like a drink?" asked Tien Lai. After ordering the first round of drinks, scotch and waters for the men and the usual cokes for the ladies, and stopped to think of it, I couldn't remember a Chinese girl yet that had ever ordered anything other than a soft drink or tea. The mood became more natural for me, as Paul began to steer the conversation. His manner was poised, and his English was perfect, just the exact image that one expects in a pilot. His masculine features bordered on the definition of being handsome, almost six feet, well built, flawlessly dressed, a flair about his personality. He, looking about twenty-five, and he and Linda made a most attractive couple.

Easing into a familiar current topic, he commented, "I hope you enjoyed your flight with us to Hualien this morning, and your trip to Taroko Gorge with Tien Lai." With deep thought, I said, "Not only did I enjoy the flight and Taroko Gorge, but more than that though, I am enjoying the hospitality of the Sheng family in making my whole day a pleasant and thoroughly complete memory." Paul responded with a tone of sincerity, "Tai Le, I hope you don't mind me being informal by calling you Tai Le. We want you to feel like you're a member of the family. You know, we Chinese are very much like you Americans. We take great pleasure in making true friendships. We hope that a long and lasting relationship can take root during your stay here."

Tien Lai echoed his sentiments by suggesting a toast to his brother-in-law's words. "May we find understanding between your 'grass roots' and our 'bamboo shoots.' Hao bu hao?"

"Tien Lai, Paul, Linda, and Jennifer, I've never heard an offer of friendship expressed as well. I accept." I did with a big lump in my throat and a tremendous feeling of pride, as Tien Lai raised his glass, saying, "Sui bien." At this moment, this Chinese saying of "as you like it" really rang true. It gave the toasters the freedom of choice in demonstrating the real feeling for their commitment. A polite sip in this case is really as false as our Western custom of gusto in saying "down the hatch." The real feeling of the toast was expressed in the way they held their glass or cup. The direct glance of the eyes, the lingering sip from the cup of togetherness, "sui bien" in this case was certainly received and given with every sense of feeling for a long and lasting cultural relationship, and the bonds were sealed between East and West.

A rapport between the five of us rapidly developed, uninterrupted by the events of a fine meal. I hadn't even noticed that Tien Lai had done the ordering for us. The meal in this very Western Restaurant decor was excellent. European cuisine, the appetizers of onion soup, and the entrée of fondue seemed to blend right into and set the mood for our social enjoyment.

Our conversations ranging from the levity of comparing our Oriental versus Western stereotyped images of male and female beauty, to the gravity of Confucism versus Christianity were challenging both comparing and defending the basic values, each of our own ancestry. "You know," I remarked, "we Occidentals and you Orientals have through our history felt that our worlds, cultures, and values are as we are geographically, at opposite ends of the earth. I, for one, believe that our hearts and minds may say the words differently but the meaning is the same. Take our proverb, 'all good things come to an end,' and you say, 'Life is not an everlasting banquet.' Do you agree, we, as basic peoples, have more in common than we give ourselves credit for?"

It was clear that all of us understood and more importantly felt this sense of commonality as human beings. "I agree," replied Paul. "It is so important in our complex, over-structured world of today that we understand each other, not so much as to our differences, but more as to our similarities. Hao bu hao?"

Jennifer nodded her approval and then placed her hand on mine, in open view of all, and then looked at me, her face glowing with pride. "Tai Le Hsien Sheng, your words and ---- are almost like Chinese. Would you come home with me?" Not knowing what thoughts were her intentions, everyone, including myself, waited for her next statement as she paused and then spoke again, "I mean, I want you to meet my father and mother for dinner." Tien Lai picked up the invitation, saying, "You have only one night left before you go home. Our house is open to you. Hao bu hao?"

"Hao," I replied. "It would be a real honor for me to join you and your family tomorrow. We 'Mei Gwo Ren' say a good home-cooked meal is always better than eating out." "Isn't that funny?" said Linda. "We Chinese also say that typical native food can only be found at home."

As the conversation shifted from the group to individuals, I found myself talking, almost in isolation from the others, solely to Jennifer. Although her English was not as polished as Linda's, she spoke with expressiveness in her face and eyes. "Tai Le Hsien Sheng, my brother has told me much about you. Even though he has not known you long, he feels he has known you for a long time. You have a good feeling for Chinese, I can tell." Suddenly switching to a dialogue of broken English, as if apologizing, but without an expression of guilt, Jennifer said, "My English is poor . . . I want to learn . . . My major in college is English and music . . . I know rules, but have not had good luck like Linda to meet man like Paul who can practice with me." Suddenly realizing she had confused her words, she blushed a little, but clarified her intentions with a laugh and a twinkle in her eyes, "Practice English, you know what I mean? Would you be my Yin Gwo Hwa lao shr . . . my teacher?"

"Jennifer, I'll make you a bargain," I replied. "If you will be my 'Chung Gwo Hwa Lao Shr (Chinese teacher),' I will be your English teacher. Hao bu hao?" "You must promise," she said, raising her little finger and gesturing for me to do the same, catching our fingers and pulling as if in a handshake. When the others noticed the extent of our involvement, Tien Lai in true brotherly fashion interrupted the bargaining session, saying, "Remember, Jennifer, as your older brother, you must Father's permission seek." When she explained, "Our promised relationship is to be one of teacher-student," Tien Lai gave his seal of approval, willingly but protecting his sister's honor, he cautioned, "Tai Le Hsien Sheng, I would have to give deep thought to any other relationship." Recognizing the humor and drama, this interplay was the signal for all to finish our dinner, and another exceptional evening of friendship came to a close, much before I wanted it to end.

CHAPTER 18

Finding Ms. Chu, Right-Hand Woman

I awoke early the following morning—anxious to begin my next-to-last day—hoping for the best, expecting the worst... in my search of my Chinese Jane Armstrong and Girl Friday: my secretary.

As I sat in the coffee shop having an early 7:00 a.m. breakfast, my mind conjured up all kinds of thought as to the prospective candidates. I could visualize a host of the more refined and experienced candidates having passed up my ad for a "sexretary" for fear that they might be working for a "foreign sex maniac" boss.

Actually what I had pictured in my lucky 7 mind was a "Miss Efficiency" who looked like Nancy Kwan, who had captured my heart in her movie role as Suzie Wong. Hoping to confirm my imagination, I looked around the coffee shop. Usually several beauties came for breakfast each morning; it normally helped to start my day off right. As I looked around, my hopes were dampened... all of the five Oriental females seated in the dining room this morning were hopelessly caught in their middle-age spread, wrinkled and generally looking like sixty-year-old men. I chuckled to myself as my visions of the perfect loveliness vanished, and I came to a strange realization: in all of my two and half years in Japan and now one week in China, had I ever seen an Oriental woman over fifty that could compare to some of the Occidental Marlene Dietrichs or Dinah Shores?

Glancing at my watch, noting that it was now eight o'clock, I paid my bill and proceeded to head straight for the offices of the *China Post* to pick up the resumes that would be my clues to selection of probably one of the most important members of my staff. Strangely, the streets this morning were very orderly and business-like as I made the ten-minute trek from the hotel to the newspaper with an editorial character.

As I approached the entrance of the *China Post*, the sight of the Hilton Hotel caught my attention and aroused a humorous reflection of my prior naivety . . . now much more mature in the ways of the Orient. I wondered if I'd ever muster the courage to go through the whole routine. "Another time," I convinced myself, as I opened the door to my favorite newspaper.

Miss Chao, the want-ads playwright, greeted me with a most warm "Dzao" and a shy but pleasant smile asking, "Tai Le Hsien Sheng, ni hao ma?" Without giving me a chance to answer, she turned and darted into an office and returned as quickly with a package . . . which she placed on the counter. Almost as if she were giving me a Christmas present, she waited to see if I was going to open it. Thinking that I'd better look to make sure I had the right package, I slowly proceeded to open the envelope and remove the contents. The pile of resumes must have been at least twenty-five in number, and as Miss Chao watched me quickly leaf through them, her eyes grew big and her face beamed with obvious pleasure and she exclaimed, "So much people like to work for you. I am so happy!" Then she pleaded in all seriousness, Please talk to Miss Chu . . . my friend . . . you will like . . . I ask her apply."

Confident that the package was mine and pleased with the volume of applicants, I knew I had a full day's work ahead of me. Miss Chao watched my face intently waiting to sense my mood, so I looked at her and said, "Chao Shiao Jai, you have done a fine job for me. I promise I will talk to your Miss Chu. Hsieh hsieh Nin." Then I turned to leave, saying, "Dzai jen, dzai jen." Her face glowed with pride, and I thought to myself as I walked back to the hotel, "I hope all of my employees are as eager as Miss Chao . . . might even be worth the thought of offering her a job when the right time comes." I walked briskly back to the hotel ... anxious to sit down to review the candidates applications.

Sitting in my room, I made a quick pass review of the resumes and tallied twenty-four applicants. My cursory look revealed that only six could be considered seriously. Most of the rejects lacked even the most basic of prior secretarial experience. Many of the resumes were incomplete and showed their obvious lack of command of the English language, with inaccurate sentence structure and poor grammar and spelling. Each and every one did, however, include a picture, and I chuckled as I looked at one ... a schoolgirl picture of a rather plain girl in a typical bowl-style school haircut and another somewhat incongruous for the typically reserved Chinese women, from a sweet but nicely built young thing ... who obviously had taken the ad seriously and provided a reserved bathing suit pose ... one piece—not bikini. I studied the resumes of the six ... tentatively acceptable candidates ... in great detail, and much to my pleasure, I found the resume of the recommended Miss Chu to be one of the most likely prospects.

Promptly, I decided to call each of the six to talk with them, with the end objective being to arrange for an interview if the outcome of the phone conversation revealed that they were, in fact, qualified and most importantly ... really interested. This exercise proved to be a most valuable step in the interview process as I promptly proceeded to eliminate three of the six not having the command of the English language that I had set as my standard for a passing rating.

The three candidates who came through with flying colors were Mrs. Tao, Miss Wei, and again, much to my surprise and mounting curiosity, Miss Chu. Both Mrs. Tao and Miss Chu presented excellent credentials and unimpeachable references. Mrs. Tao, who was in her early 40s, but whose picture looked like an Oriental Lauren Bacall, had a most intriguing background, with fifteen years' experience as a secretary, the last ten of which were as personal secretary to the Chief of Staff of the US Military Advisory Assistance Group and was married to a Chinese Brigadier General. She sounded, as we talked, like she was a very well-organized, mature person. We agreed to meet at noon for lunch in the lobby of the Orchid Room of the hotel.

Miss Wei's resume looked like a long-shot, but worth pursuing. Short on experience with only two years as a secretary to a department head of a local—and rival—US electronics firm, the major assets of her portfolio being that of a college degree with a major in English and a minor in journalism from an English university in Hong Kong, and the picture revealed her most attractive feature . . . she was beautiful! Her face looked vaguely familiar, but when I asked her on the phone, she replied, "No, I don't think we've met." She was a most interesting conversationalist as we talked, and she explained that she was interested in the opportunity of advancement. Miss Wei asked that we meet about three o'clock in my hotel room so our meeting would not be an open advertisement to her interest in switching jobs. Cautious about such an arrangement, but not wanting to jeopardize her employment status, I reluctantly agreed.

Miss R. I. Chu answered my call with a most pleasant yet business-like greeting, demonstrating her professional capability. She was obviously caught in the presence of her boss, but very cordially apologized for being busy and asked if she could return my call at my convenience. "Quick-thinking in a tight spot," was my immediate conclusion. When she called back within the half hour, she again apologized, explaining the situation that she had been taking dictation and that today was a very busy day—the monthly reports to the home office were due out today. She asked if I could possibly arrange to meet later in the day. Since she was also concerned about a public showing, we agreed to meet at 6:00 p.m. at the new-to-be ABC office, suggesting that she'd like to see what our new offices looked like. Her professional credentials were most impressive—ten years as an executive secretary with two foreign investment firms . . . one USA and the other Dutch. I thought to myself, "If she can satisfy a Dutchman, who are noted as being tyrants for work, she must be good." Her picture reflected her to be a very beautiful woman with a soft, doe-eyed look. Looking at her resume again, I wondered if the deck wasn't being stacked in her favor, when I noticed her resume references looked somewhat like a Who's Who List of my social and business contacts, starting with Minister Tseng, Editor-in-Chief Nancy Wang of the *China Post*, Chairman Chiang of my new bank . . . the Tai Fong, and none other than Tien Lai Tseng.

Noon . . . time for my first interview rolled around quickly . . . so, off I went to meet Mrs. Tao.

Interested in making a favorable impression on this woman—my senior in age—I developed a very gentlemanly frame of mind to 1) be on time and 2) be respectful, but casually dominant. My mental role was quickly disrupted when, without apology, she appeared thirty minutes late and introduced herself with an arm-shattering handshake. "I'm Louise Tao, and you are Mr. Trailer, I presume?" She wasn't exactly dressed in a military tunic, but her high-neck collar and loose-fitting sack-style dress and her cold, hard, penetrating look gave her the appearance of an Army colonel at basic training camp talking to one of her recruits.

"Come, Mr. Toiler, let's have some lunch," she suggested. She led and I followed her into the plush surroundings of the Orchid Room to find us seated at a table within full view of numerous Chinese businessmen and US military brass. It didn't take me five minutes as she proceeded to tell me, "Take the Golden Fried Shrimp, you'll like them," . . . to figure out that she wanted to run ABC. I got one question into the conversation asking, "Mrs. Tao, why do you want to leave your present job, which would appear to be a very responsible . . ." Before I could finish the question, she answered curtly, "Because I'm at the top of my salary range of RMB$10,000, per year, and I know US companies pay much more than the US military." The rest of the lunch hour, she led the conversation not because I wanted to listen, because she wasn't about to let me interrupt.

As I listened, I watched this "Mata Hari" with fascination. She was most intriguing. Her intense piercing looks went clear through me. She sat on the edge of her seat, her lunch growing cold as she looked at me straight in the eyes and continued, "Mr. Tai Le." She got the name right one out of ten times. "I run the office of my boss—the Chief of Staff of MAAG. I've been there ten years now, and I've had to train four US major generals. Now I'm on my fifth one. They leave all the administrative responsibility to me. You know, I have 'Top Secret' security clearance. I can guarantee you that I know all the right people in the right places in the Chinese government. My husband used to be on Generalissimo Chiang Kai Shek's staff. That's why I would be indispensable to you. My bosses usually leave everything to me and play golf at least three afternoons per week."

Finally spotting an opportunity, I asked an academic question, "Mrs. Tao, how's your shorthand?" Rather quickly, she replied, "It's fine, but I haven't used it for over three years now. I prefer to have my boss use a dictaphone or give me a pencil draft." Dropping the skills portion of my interview tactics, I proceeded to prolong the conversation to tell her about ABC. When I came to the part about "You know, our plant is to be built out near Chung Li—about a one and half hour drive each way out of the metropolitan city" and before I could tell her that bus transportation would be provided by the company, she interrupted, "Oh, that's OK with me. I won't mind, as long as you send a car and driver after me." Knowing that she now worked a five-day, forty-hour a week for Uncle Sam, I hesitated to break the news to her about our plans for a six-day, forty-eight-hour week schedule.

During the course of her conversation, I'd come to a basic conclusion that I didn't need an office general-dictator-type as a secretary. Hell, I wanted to manage the operation and the people. But, not knowing what my other prospects were like, I thought it best that I keep the prospect alive before telling her that she didn't fit into my plans. So, I fibbed a little, as I told her, "Mrs. Tao, I sincerely appreciate your interest in ABC and the chance to talk about the executive secretary position. You know, I feel this position to be one of the most important on my staff." Her mouth opened, and she began to comment, but I managed to keep the advantage, saying, "I do want you to know that I have a number of other candidates to interview before I make my choice. I will plan to call you tomorrow to give you my decision."

Clearly, I had hurt her feelings. As we walked out of the dining room, she looked at me again with her best cold, hard glance, saying, "You know, Mr. Tai Le, I don't know why you even plan to waste your precious time. I'm the best secretary available." I had to bite the inside of my cheek hard to keep from emitting a noticeable laugh and grin, but with my best diplomatic effort, I responded, "Mrs. Tao, I don't doubt your confidence, but I feel it's only fair to talk to as many candidates as possible. Who knows, I might find some secretarial talent for my department heads." Not wanting to leave with the last word, she regained her composure attempting to impress me with her indispensable repertoire of skills, "Don't worry about hiring secretaries or department heads. I'm quite capable of finding and hiring all the people you'll need." And with that she turned and walked away, with a noticeable swagger to her steps.

    I felt relieved as I got back to my hotel room, wondering what the next two interviews were going to be like. With about an hour before Miss Wei's scheduled appearance, I decided to make several promised phone calls. The first was to C. C. Chiu of the Tai Fong Bank to let Chairman Chiang know of my interest in accepting his offer to locate my new offices at their Shanghai South Road branch bank. C. C. was most pleased with our decision which he promised to report immediately to Chairman Chiang. His pleasure was conveyed in an invitation to another dinner outing at the Sincere Hotel in Peitou. "Thanks," I replied. "I already have a dinner tonight. How about a rain check for later, when I return with my family?" Jokingly, he asked, "If you can get permission from your 'tai-tai' to go to Peitou? Hen hao!" Concluding our conversation, he agreed to advise Mr. Wu, at the branch, of my plans to visit there for my six o'clock interview with Miss Chu.

    Next, I decided to call Peter Huang of the Tenth Commercial Bank to advise him of my decision, obviously unfavorable to his bank's interests. As I thanked him for their interests in the ABC account, I also felt it appropriate to express my appreciation for their hospitality at dinner in the Mandarin Palace. His response pleased me as he stated the bank's philosophy, "We, at the Tenth Commercial Bank, are disappointed that we have failed to demonstrate that we can provide the best banking services for your company ABC. We remain confident that we can be of service and would like the pleasure of paying an occasional call to your office after you begin operations in your new plant. Business is never so small that it cannot justify the use of more than one good bank." I thought, as we said our "Dzai Jens," the theory of "Oriental loss of face" sure hadn't held true in this case.

Wanting to wrap up my last piece of unfinished business before my three o'clock interview, I placed a call to Henry Chao, to set into motion the legal actions for ABC's foreign investment application and corporate registration and to work out a lease agreement with Lodge Right and Mr. Tze for my "Shangrila" in the rice fields. I was reassured, again, to have Henry tell me, "Don't worry about anything. Action on your FIA is already underway. I'll write to you every two weeks in the USA, so you know how everything is going."

No sooner than we had finished, my doorbell rang. As I proceeded to answer, I felt very confident that everything was going well. Now, if only I could find my Girl Friday to take care of getting my offices set up in my absence. As I opened the door, my personal confidence took a mild setback. There in the doorway stood a true beauty, Oriental or otherwise. Wish confidence and poise, she said, "Good afternoon, Mr. Tai Le. I'm Simone Wei." Stuttering a bit, slightly at a loss for words, wondering if my pure business-like interview technique was about to be compromised, I blushed and said, "Glad to see you again, Miss Wei. Won't you come in?" This time, it was her turn to be on the defensive as she looked puzzled at my statement, trying to recollect the significance of my use of the word, "again."

"I knew your photo reminded me that I had seen you before. Although we haven't officially met, perhaps you'll remember seeing me at the Queens Restaurant last week?" Gambling on an embarrassing situation developing, I asked, "I did see you there, didn't I?" Visibly shaken, her face flushed. It was obvious her "undercover" occupation had come out into the open Exercising discretion, as well as all of her feminine guile, she broke into tears, saying, "I'm very sorry, that I have attempted to fool you." And with that, she headed for the door. Not wanting to let the whole episode end without a full explanation, I stepped in front of her, gently grabbing her arm to stop her. Before I could say, "Miss Wei, please sit and let's talk," she was leaning on me and crying gently on my shoulder. My instinctive reaction was to back away. Then I found myself liking the thought of her in my arms and I'll have to be honest, I considered whether I should take advantage of the situation, but finally with somewhat of a guilty conscience on that idea, I realized that she needed a father figure.

Looking out the room window at the city below, I spoke to her softly, "Simone, look out at the world. Life is a lot like what you see out there. The sunshine brings a lot of hope and happiness into our lives. But the sun doesn't always shine and we have to learn to live with the rain and the darkness. You, too, have to learn to live your life under all kinds of personal weather conditions." Pausing to reflect on what I had said, she then stepped back, looked at me with her big beautiful, but still moist eyes, she said very sweetly, "Thank you for your comforting presence. Can I still talk with you about the job?" "Sure," I answered. "Let's sit down and talk." "Please," she responded, "first I'd like to dry my eyes and fix my makeup. May I?"

While she took a few minutes to get herself together, I ordered a couple of Cokes from room service. She came out of the bathroom, with all the poise and carriage of "Miss China," and we sat down and talked. For the first time, since she had walked in, I became fully aware of the sophistication, feminine charm, and physical beauty of Simone. She radiated, as she spoke, "You know what I am in the hours of darkness, but I want you to know what I am when the sun shines. I'm not proud of the fact that I've taken to playing games with all kinds of men, but I'll be frank and say that I'm in it for the money. I make about US$150 as a secretary. I enjoy my work, and I believe that I'm a good secretary. I make between US$500-$750 a month at the Queens. I am also good at that job, but I don't enjoy anything about the work, except the money."

"Let me ask a leading question, Simone. When will you quit? Now or when you feel you have enough money, or when you're too old to be enjoyed for men's fancies?" She didn't beat around the bush answering, "I have two objectives in life. The first is to find a respectable job in which I can earn a decent living, and after I accomplish that objective, then I want to find a man who is interested in loving me as a person, not for my reputation as a lover, but is interested in having a family."

Repeating my leading question, I asked, "Simone, I must know, are you ready to quit now?" A warm and responsive smile came to her beautiful face and her eyes glistened as she replied with surprise, "Mr. Tai Le, are you offering to fulfill my second objective?" "No, Simone," I responded. "As much as I'd be pleased to attempt to fulfill that role, I am a happily married man. What I was leading up to is the requirement of my executive secretary. I don't want this to sound like I'm moralizing, because normally I don't feel it's any of my business as to how, why, or where my employees spend their hours after work, just as long as they get their job done, well. In this position, however, your 'moonlight' occupation would present a conflict of interests. Many of our customers and executives from the USA will want to work hard during the day and play hard at night. Right or wrong, although the men will consider their escapades, in the absence of their families, as totally acceptable behavior, your dual employment with ABC, in a responsible position by day, and at the Queens, as an entertainer by night, would be considered as a violation of moral ethics."

Looking at me softly, her eyes reflected her understanding and her voice did not reflect the indignation I'm sure she felt in her heart, as she softly spoke, "Mr. Tai Le, as you know, I do not feel that I can afford to quit now. With my present job, I am not in the direct focus and cause no one embarrassment by my dual role, although it is known by my fellow Chinese employees. It is obvious then that I must give up my interest in your opportunity, since I cannot relinquish my own personal objectives for income for at least two to three more years." As she stood up, she once again caused me to glance longingly at her, but this time I saw more than just her beautiful physical features. I saw her as a complete person, intelligent, resourceful, and understanding. Quite a woman.

"I hope I haven't disappointed you, Simone. You haven't disappointed me. You're much more of a person than I think you give yourself credit for." "Thank you, Mr. Tai Le," she said. Then taking my hand, she maneuvered close to me and standing on her tip-toes, she kissed me on the cheek. "You give me much happiness today. Money cannot buy that."

Her eyes sparkled as she let go of my hand, and she walked to the door. "One day," she said with pride, "I will return the same measure of happiness to you." And with a wink and a good-bye, she was gone.

Reflecting on the experience was a pleasant, but momentary memory. I grew concerned when I collected my thoughts. Two interview pitches, two strikes. One more and I'm out. I found myself wishing and hoping, almost as if in prayer, that my interview with Miss Chu would be an answer to my Girl Friday problem. So I hurried down to the street entrance to the hotel, anxious to catch a cab for our new, but empty offices.

With the assistance of the doorman, giving my cab driver instructions as to my destination, I was speeding off for my next interview rendezvous. For some reason, I had a good feeling about the outcome.

Although it was a few minutes before six o'clock when I arrived, Miss Chu was there waiting for me. Immediately, it was obvious that the old cliché "The third time's a charm" was to be proven true again. Although we were total strangers, there was no difficulty in recognizing each other as we first met. My first impression was extremely positive: She was quite attractive, much better looking than her resume picture, obviously very mature and poised, yet with a shy, subtle, and reserved quality. Tall for a Chinese woman, she had a radiant appearance with sparkle in her eyes and warmth in her smile, dressed with fashionable taste in a canary-yellow shift, conservative, not too revealing, but properly accentuating her shapely figure.

Our introduction was simple. She softly announced, "Good evening, Mr. Tai Le. I'm Chu Ru Ing. I use the given name of

Rita." I replied, in Chinese, "Chu Shiao Jai, nin hao ma? Waw shing Tai Le Lo Pu." Although she did not fluster like so many Chinese when an Occidental speaks to them in their native tongue, it was obvious she was pleased with my attempt. We stood looking at each other for a few seconds, but what seemed to be an hour, oblivious to the pedestrians and heavy, noisy traffic on the streets. The chemistry was perfect and a mutually satisfying feeling came obvious as we looked at each other. Then, almost as if in syncopation, we spoke simultaneously, saying, "Shall we go into the office?" Finding the bank's doors locked, Miss Chu looked for a side entrance, which she found in the narrow alleyway. A bank employee responded to her ringing of a special doorbell and let us in. Miss Chu, in a very business-like manner, explained in Chinese that we wanted to gain access to ABC's new offices on the third floor. Within seconds, Mr. Wu, the branch manager, came, and upon recognizing me, introduced himself, in Chinese, and welcomed us. Then, with a great deal of pomp and circumstance, he escorted the two of us to our office and proudly proceeded to hand me the keys. He gave us a grand tour of our three small office units, and then the bank employee's recreation facilities, explaining to Miss Chu that they, too, were available to us to use and enjoy.

Then he left us to explore our new office space. Demonstrating her self-confidence and initiative, Miss Chu, very diplomatically, took charge. She began to ask questions about, "How many people will we plan to locate here? How long will we plan to use these offices? When will our plan in Nei Li be ready? What kind of furniture and decorations would I like? Could she arrange to bring in a contractor to clean, paint, and brighten up the dull, drab appearance of the office?"

Within the next ten minutes, I realized it really wasn't necessary to go through the normal routine of an interview. I liked her references to our . . . her company. The professional efficiency of Miss Chu was most obvious. When I asked her, "Do you feel capable of setting up and managing the offices during my absence?" she replied with a subtle, but confident, "I hope to be the most dependable and capable member of your staff." When I asked her, "What do you feel to be one of the most important attributes of a secretary?" She responded with gentle pride, "Loyalty to her boss." Explaining to her that many activities like opening bank accounts, contacting lawyers, talking to government officials, and setting up our accounting books ought to be accomplished before my return in eight weeks, she volunteered her immediate services, saying, "If you need me now, I'd be pleased to take off from work until you leave. However, Mr. Tai Le, I hope you will understand," she said, "that I must do the right thing with my present employer. If I resign, I feel obligated to give them at least one month's notice, but I will work for you in the evenings to make sure everything goes as you wish."

Convinced that her professional skills need not be questioned any further, I expressed, "Miss Chu, I . . ." She gently interrupted with a questioning look at me, "Please feel free to call me Rita." "Rita," I began again, "one thing which I feel very important—I want to learn how to speak Chinese. Will you be my teacher?" "I would be honored," she said in a humble manner. "You have learned much already, and your accent is good," she complimented. Almost embarrassed by her praise, I apologized, "Not really, my ability is poor, but I am anxious to learn." With that, she offered me her little finger, which she hooked with mine, saying, "Good, we will seal the bargain. This is a promise in Chinese."

At this point, it was apparent that I should make her a formal offer. "Rita," I began, "I'd like to ask you to become my secretary, but I'm sure you would like to think about it and give me an answer later." Her face shone, reflecting the pleasure of the moment, and she spoke confidently yet with an unusual gentleness, "Mr. Tai Le, I do not need to hesitate on my decision. I accept." "But," I stammered, "we haven't even begun to establish the salary and benefits." Again, she replied directly, "I am not concerned. The satisfaction I know that I will have in working for you and the challenge of my work are more important than the offer of compensation. I trust that you will establish a salary that is equal to my worth to you." Then with a beautiful smile, she asked with a simple, "Hao bu hao?" if I were agreeable to such an agreement. Replying "ding hao," I offered a handshake to seal the arrangement.

She took the initiative to hail a cab for me and accepted with some reluctance to join me as I offered to see her home. I continued to plead with gentle persuasion until I won, saying, "We can use the time to discuss a schedule of things to be accomplished during my absence." On that basis, she accepted the ride. We rode in silence for a little while after she gave the driver instructions to her home, but the longer we were together, the more of a feeling of satisfaction came over me. It was nice to know that during my two months absence to return to the United States, I would be able to rely upon Rita with complete confidence to get the job done.

My silent focus of attention to her physical attractiveness began to generate more sparks than my conscience would allow, so I asked, "Rita, do you have plans to get married in the future?" "Oh, yes," she said, "I am already married." "But," I exclaimed, "you use the 'Miss' title or address! If you're married, why don't you use 'Mrs.'?" "Women have preferred to use their maiden name for centuries in China, rather than assume the husband's family name, which is common in your country. In this way, we retain our identity with our family name, which the Western woman forfeits." "That's interesting," I concluded. "In a way, you've achieved a degree of women's liberation that only just recently our Western women have begun to struggle for." "Remember, that China has been giving to the world from our culture for over five thousand years," she emphasized.

"Tell me, then, how did you adopt the name of Rita?" I inquired. "Mr. Tai Le, most of us, who have at one time attended the missionary schools, were given a phonetic name in English, much like the Chinese name you have, Tai Le sounds like Tai Le. Ni jr dau? In Chinese, that is saying, 'Do you understand?' Hao bu hao?" Her manner of teaching me to listen to her Chinese was pleasant, and I proudly replied, "Waw jr dau. Hao bu hao?" I knew from her smile that I was on the right track. "Rita," I continued, "what does your name Chu Ru Ing mean?" She began to blush as she answered, "'Beauty like music' is the literal translation, but I do not believe it is true." Attempting to lead me away from the point, she hurried into her explanation, "In China, it is common for the girls to be given a poetical name, while the boys are named with titles of bravery and strength. I was given the name Rita by the nuns who taught at the Provident College, where I went to school." The longer she talked, the more convincing she became that her name Chu Ru Ing, "Beauty like music," was a perfect description of her character.

I could sense our rapport, a professional body chemistry, developing as we glanced at each other. Curiosity within me, as to how she had decided without hesitation that she wanted to work for ABC, prompted me to direct a question to her. "Rita, why are you so confident that you want to work for ABC and me?" She blushed a pleasant shade of crimson and then returned a shy glance to me saying, "I have talked to many people who have met you. They all give you a number one recommendation, but my decision was confirmed because of your feet." Somewhat startled as to her logic, chuckling as I looked at the comparative size of my shoe to hers, I could only project a "Why my feet?" "Chinese people," she said, "believe that a person with big feet is a very stable person, so your shoe size tells me you will be a good boss." Laughing at the analogy, I reacted with a positive, "I'll try to justify your faith."

With a few simple directions to the cab driver, we arrived at her house, in a very nice residential area of Taipei. Knowing that I was scheduled to leave at noon the next day, she volunteered, "Tai Le Hsien Sheng, could I be of help to you tomorrow? Maybe I could take off from my job tomorrow morning and meet you at the new office to work out a schedule of things to be accomplished before you return with your family in August to Taipei." "Rita," I remarked, "you know, you're already one step ahead of me. Thanks for the thought. If we could meet at eight o'clock for a couple of hours, that would be great. Hau bu hao?"

"Hen hao," was her quick response, and she got out of the cab with a smile and said, "Dzai jen, mein tien jen, a?" (See you tomorrow; OK.)

As the cab pulled away, I felt very satisfied with the way things had turned out, and as I looked back, I saw her standing there waving good-bye. I thought about my interview experiences and chuckled to myself. The range of choices, from Louise, the dictator, and Simone, the seductive temptress, to the ideal, Rita, with all the qualities I had hoped for and a person of diplomatic character.

Chapter 19

Enjoying a Real Family

Tien Lai was waiting in the lobby of the hotel when I returned. Looking at my watch, I realized it was already past the seven o'clock time that I had promised to meet him. He apparently sensed my moment of happiness as he guessed, "From the look on your face, I must assume that you have hired a secretary." "Tien Lai," I replied, "I'm not sure whether or not my choice was predestined or that I had any choice, since your name was used as a reference by Miss Chu. But, I will say that I am most pleased that she was interested in ignoring the crude reference to my need for a Sexretary. She appears to be an ideal choice. Thanks for your assistance." He smiled and nodded.

"Tien Lai, can I ask you for a couple more minutes? I have a package to get from my room," I explained, "so let me go up to the room and I will be right back."

Within minutes, Tien Lai and I were in a taxi, speeding merrily on our way to his home. Subconsciously, I looked forward to my first experience of being entertained in a Chinese home. "Tell me a little bit about your family, Tien Lai." Replying to my question, he started slowly. "Tonight, you will meet my father and mother. Of course, you know the twins, Linda and Jennifer. I have two other sisters and four other brothers, all of whom are younger than the twins and I. I should warn you about my father. He is definitely old-fashioned in a classical Chinese sense. He has a very strong will and fancies himself as an amateur philosopher. I think it would be safe to say that many of his thoughts and ways are old-fashioned and very difficult for me and my brothers and sisters to accept . . . but I respect him very much. My mother is the typical Chinese wife and mother who, although is very quiet and reserved in her manner, is really the guiding force within our family. She has a very open mind, and we children find it easy to talk to her. She is very understanding and sympathetic to our new generation's thoughts and ideas. I guess that one might say that she is the thread that holds the family together."

While still in the process of describing his family, our cab arrived. The main entrance was very unassuming and humble, but through the gate my glances reflected upon a comfortable home in a quiet residential area which obviously belonged to a middle- to upper-level income family. As we entered the gate, one had a feeling of going through a transition from the hustle-bustle routine of everyday life in China into a quiet sanctuary almost shut out from the outside world. The grounds surrounding the house were very limited, but it was obvious that painstaking care and planning had been taken to develop a beautifully landscaped garden environment. The shrubs and flowers about the house and yard were manicured with precision, and there were many flowers in bloom. Toward the back of the house was a patio area equipped with outdoor furniture of bamboo and rattan. I remarked, "I'm sure that one could spend many pleasant hours sitting here and enjoying the solitude of nature." "Ah, yes," replied Tien Lai. "My father enjoys spending his leisure time outdoors. It gives him the opportunity to contemplate the relationship of the world around him and us as a family. We . . . as a family . . . can look forward to his many philosophies of life when he returns to the house from his garden."

I enjoyed the pleasure . . . again . . . of being greeted at the front door by both Linda and Jennifer. I could see that tonight was to be a special occasion, as both of them were dressed in the classical Chinese Chi Pou dress. Both girls looked more beautiful than I had remembered. Their first gesture of hospitality was to introduce me to all of the other members of the family who were seated in the living room around their father. The presence of the nine children was somewhat overwhelming. Jennifer introduced me to her father, Sheng Wen Tsun, and he quickly rose from his chair. Taking this opportunity, I offered a small gift to Mr. Sheng, which he accepted graciously and then set aside. His apparent disregard for the gift threw me off-balance, but I caught Tien Lai's eye wink to signal that his father's gesture would be explained at a more convenient time. He extended his hand. His handshake was firm and warm. As he grasped my elbow and pulled me close to him, I could hear him express a welcome in Chinese, "Huan ying."

Mr. Sheng was very tall for a Chinese man and built very slightly. His snow-white hair revealed his age, which I guessed to be about sixty. His face carried a very warm and broad smile, and his eyes radiated with a greeting of friendship. He was dressed in a traditional full-length gown of brocaded blue silk with a high-neck collar, typical of the pictures of the Mandarin court officials. I observed him as he spoke to me in warm, friendly tones ... in Chinese ... to be every part of the picture that Tien Lai had described. His image reflected that of a sage and wise old philosopher, but yet his motions were those of a young man.

Mrs. Sheng stood dutifully by her husband's side, waiting for him to fulfill his duties as the host in greeting their guest. She, too, wore a Mandarin-style gown of Chinese red. When I finally shook hands with her, she very humbly and quietly nodded her head and looked at me with very understanding eyes. She promptly proceeded to ask each of the children to present themselves for introduction and announced them each by name. Although her manner was quiet, her appearance confirmed the image that one perceives of a person of patience, understanding, and love. Although her years had given way to an appearance of matronliness, it was obvious that in her youth, she had been a beautiful woman.

Each of her children, in their own way, reflected the strength and features of their mother and father. A few of the children ... with courage ... attempted to try out their limited knowledge of English, with a few simple words like, "Welcome, Mr. Tai Le," and "I'm pleased to meet you."

When all of the introductions had been completed, the confusion of the masses once again became regimented to an obvious family discipline. Mr. Sheng began to speak slowly, allowing Tien Lai to translate his words into English. "Mr. Tai Le," he said, "it is with a great deal of pride and honor that I welcome you, my son's friend, to our home. Tien Lai has told us much about you, and we feel as if we already know you. We accept you as a friend of the family. He has told us that you have, in many ways, a philosophy which is more Chinese than Western. Your offering of a gift to our family, that of Chinese custom . . . this act seems to confirm my son's wisdom and judgment in evaluating your character." Tien Lai, in his translation, added the reasoning for his father's act of putting the gift aside, saying, "I believe it is American custom to open the gift in front of the giver and voicing words of admiration. Chinese custom is to open the gift in the absence of the giver, but I assure you that the gift is received with a great sense of appreciation."

At that moment, Mr. Sheng suggested that we all sit down around a circular coffee table to enjoy a toast to our friendship. Clapping his hands was the signal for one of the servants to approach the table and extend a bottle to Mr. Sheng. Tien Lai translated, "This wine which my father offers you is a very special wine called Da Chiu. It is a product of the island of Kinmen, which most westerners refer to as Quemoy, and is an extraction from the sorghum plant. By Oriental standards, Western liquor and wine are impotent. Da Chiu is 180 proof and one must drink it with care." Mr. Sheng proceeded to pour glasses for himself, Tien Lai, and me. Linda, Jennifer, Mrs. Sheng, and the children all appeared to be satisfied to accept a Coke for their part in participating in this toast of welcome. With a "Gam Bai," I took my first taste of Chinese "White Lightning." The effect was immediate: my eyes moistened, and within seconds, I could feel my earlobes taking on a radiant glow. "Hau bu hau?" asked the elder Sheng. "Hen Hao," was my quick reply. Before I had a chance to set my wine glass down, I was promptly offered a refill. Tien Lai cautioned his father kiddingly, speaking so that I too could understand. "BaBa, man man de, a?" Strangely, I translated his "slow down" signal to his father as the same caution sign frequently issued to taxicab drivers, but I also sensed that the elder Mr. Sheng was solidly in command of the situation, despite his son's words of warning.

Mr. Sheng immediately took command of the conversation. He proceeded to ask me fundamental questions about myself, all of which was in due process translated by Tien lai. It was evident that I was being closely analyzed and evaluated as he inquired, "Where were your parents born? What does your father do? Where were you born? How were you educated? Do you have brothers and sisters? Do you speak any other languages? What was your business background and experience prior to coming to China? How old are you? Are you married and how many children do you have? Are your parents still living, and do they live in your home?"

Again, through Tien Lai, I explained, "I am one of two sons, a twin, born of German-immigrant parents who came to the United States. I have a university education. I was married at the age of twenty-two and now have three children. The two oldest of which are two boys born in Japan." I sensed a chuckle in his reaction as I told him, "I have a younger twin brother." His humorous look turned to one of satisfaction as I explained, "I worked my way through school to get a college degree," and then shifted again to a frown when I told him that I had married at the age of twenty-two. His face beamed at my statement that my firstborn was a son, born in the Orient. Again, he frowned as I said, "My parents live in my hometown, about five hundred miles from my family home in the state of Indiana."

Mr. Sheng collected his thoughts and pondered my answers as he looked at me ... trying to develop his overall appraisal of my character before asking me a very pointed and obvious question concerning my filial piety. "Why do your parents not live in your home?" To this, I answered, "This custom, although common in the generation prior to mine, is slowly breaking down in our society due to the increasing mobility of the family." I explained, as an example, "Although I took work in a new community away from my parents' home, an offer stands open for my parents to live with us. However, they are reluctant to move and leave their friends and community interests behind." Mr. Sheng philosophized, "This breakdown of traditional family structure should be one of great concern to the future of Western culture." My awareness of his sense of wisdom and understanding grew as he explained, "The foundation of the Chinese culture was based upon the unity of the family." In a very poetical sense, Mr. Sheng told me, "The family is like a plant . . . the father being the seed, the mother being the root, and the children being the flowers and the fruits. The origin of the family concept comes from the teachings of Confucius. Confucianism has been the governing doctrine of most of the basic aspects of life in China for many, many centuries and from it comes life . . . with its happiness and sorrow. 'Life in China can be best described through its proverbs. These proverbs originate like the plant . . . from the people of the soil . . . and express the basic principles and values of life. They have meaning to our people and are passed along from generation to generation. The wisdom found in our proverbs is not that of the scholar or the philosopher, but it is that which comes from the people of the street, the farm, and the villages. If they are crude, it is because the people who spoke them are very basic. Proverbs, as they have been called, are the "tears of humanity." They embody what the old Chinese people regarded as truth and represent their ideas of life and personal conduct.' (*700 Chinese Proverbs, 1*) Our Chinese philosophy, found in these proverbs, touches on many areas of our everyday life, including politics, education, religion, friendship, the family, and our relationships with other people. As we sit down to dinner, I would like to speak to you of some of my favorite sayings to compare the wisdom of our Chinese culture with your understanding of these same values from your culture. I am anxious to inquire as to the validity of our teachings, such that I may form an opinion of Western ways, which we have been taught to regard as being somewhat barbaric compared to the humble qualities of Chinese ideology."

It was an opportune time for Mrs. Sheng to break the conversation at this time, asking all of us to sit down for dinner. The seating arrangement, around the circular table, was again determined by the elder Mr. Sheng and, as his guest, I was seated to his left. Tien Lai, as his eldest son, was seated to his right, and the others were seated in accordance with their rank determined by age. Finally, Mrs. Sheng seated herself to my left, next to the youngest child. At Mr. Sheng's command, the maid gave him a bottle of rice wine, from which he filled my cup and Tien Lai's. He promptly offered to "Gam bei." I mentioned quietly to Tien Lai, "It appears as if your father is going to test my drinking stamina this evening." Tien Lai chuckled and said, "Yes, you're right. Please don't disappoint my father by refusing to accept his challenge. He wants to test your ability to carry the banner . . . as a member of our family . . . as to your drinking abilities in competition with his friends So it is a simple test of Western endurance versus Oriental tolerance." So, I enjoyed several toasts with gusto, but all the while hoping that we could proceed with the first course so that I could fill a very empty cavity in my stomach before the effects of the alcohol coursed through my brain.

Mrs. Sheng offered to help me with the first dish of the evening, which was presented on the lazy susan in the center of the table. It was a beautiful vegetable and Hors d'oeuvre tray done artistically with radishes carved as roses and curled carrots . . . a variety of tiny pieces of chicken, barbecued pork, fresh shrimp, and crab meat. My first reaction was to compliment Mrs. Sheng, which Jennifer translated. The result of which was a broad smile of satisfaction from her mother as she offered me a second helping.

Following the second course round of rice wine "Gam Bais," Mr. Sheng resumed his philosophical discourse as Mrs. Sheng served the second course of turtle soup. In a teasing vein, Tien Lai's father cautioned me, "Do not eat too much of the turtle meat." Asking the leading question, "Why?" was like putting one's foot in the mouth, as he explained to the laughter of his sons and the blushes of his daughters, "Turtle meat is like an aphrodisiac and is generally served to stimulate the amorous interests of the male." He even blushed a little when I asked, through Tien Lai, "How does the turtle meat affect you?" He didn't give me an answer, but he proceeded to savor his dish with obvious relish.

    The next dish was one of my favorites made of bamboo shoots, lotus roots, and black mushrooms. I commented to Mrs. Sheng, "I thoroughly enjoy bamboo shoots." This prompted the elder Mr. Sheng to offer another bit of wisdom, "When eating bamboo shoots, one should remember the person who planted them." With another toast of rice wine, which proceeded to flow more rapidly with each course, Mr. Sheng once again acknowledged me as a friend of the family saying, "To make or meet an old friend in a distant land is like the refreshing rain after a long drought." (From the *700 Chinese Proverbs*)

    The "ahma" (maid) brought the next dish which was also one of my favorites, a sweet and sour yellow fish. Upon asking Mrs. Sheng about the origin of this dish, Linda explained, "This is a typical Shanghainese dish which is also a favorite of the family." "I can honestly say," I complimented, "that I have never tasted any fish that is quite as delicious as the way that the Chinese prepare them . . . baked whole and garnished with fruits and sauces." The meat fell off the spine with a simple touch of the fork as she proceeded to serve me and her husband, letting the others take care of themselves. When I mentioned that I was amazed to find such a tremendous variety of dishes which are native to the various provinces of the mainland . . . each with a distinct and different taste . . . the elder Mr. Sheng explained, "Chinese food characterizes the different types of people within the country." Proceeding to elucidate, he continued, "The twenty two provinces of China are almost each by themselves like a different country. Notice if you will that the first fact to be established when two Chinese people meet each other is to identify the other's native province. The Chinese do this because they have characterized and stereotyped each other based upon where they were born. For example, people from Shanghai are generally regarded to be the most successful Chinese in the professional fields of business endeavor. Most of the bankers and lawyers have been born, reared, and educated in Shanghai. People from Peiping are regarded as the most educated and scholarly of the Chinese and most representative of the Mandarin culture. As you know, their dialect has been accepted as the standard for the Chinese language. People from the provinces of Shansi and Shensi, as northern people, are considered the most amorous of the Chinese people. The Shantungese are considered to be the most determined, honest, and stubborn people, but not regarded as having a high degree of intellect. People from the interior provinces of Hopei, Hopeh, and Szechuan most generally have become the warriors, soldiers, and generals in our history. Our Cantonese have been our merchants and missionaries throughout the world. Most foreigners consider them as representatives of all of our peoples. In fact, most of the Chinese who have immigrated to other countries, such as your China Towns of the USA, are of the Cantonese origin." Mr. Sheng continued to explain, "Chinese also have distinctly different physical and personality characteristics distinguished by their native origin."

I found his analogy of the differences within the Chinese to be very typical of the differences in the Occidental whose cultures stem from the European continent. I attempted to explain to him, "The Europeans are also characterized very similarly . . . based upon their geographic origin. As an example . . . the Italians and Greeks have provided the basic roots of our culture, but are presently characterized as being the lovers of the European peoples. The Germans, like your Shantungese, with traits of stubbornness, are also like your soldiers from Hopei. The English, by like token, have been regarded as the scholars, and the Nordic and Scandinavians as the most peaceful and productive. Each of these nations has also been characterized as having distinct physical and personality stereotyped images." Mr. Sheng appeared to be very engrossed in absorbing my explanation of the similarities between the two countries and then commented, "Perhaps there has been, somewhere in past history, a link between the two cultures. Most likely transferred from China by our Marco Polo." I winked to him rather diplomatically.

Accepting the compliment humbly, he continued, "My son tells me and I observe that you are making an effort to learn our language, and for this I must compliment you. We have a saying, 'when in a foreign country, if you want to know the people, speak the language of that place.' (*700 Chinese Proverbs*) In truth, it is only when you can understand the language that you become familiar with the true nature of the people, their customs, their traditions, their superstitions."

In response to Mr. Sheng's proposal of a toast, I answered his comment with some embarrassment, attempting, in Chinese, to tell him that, "Truly I speak very little Chinese." He was pleased with this statement, in that it reflected an expression of humbleness. He remarked, "You speak with humility, which is also typical of our people."

Mrs. Sheng beckoned to the servants for the next dish to be served, which I recognized immediately as the Chinese dumpling . . . Chiao Tze. As I expressed my pleasure to Mrs. Sheng, Mr. Sheng proceeded to explain, "This dish is typical of northern China and in particular, in the area of the capital, Peiping. It was the custom in this part of the country that when one was invited as a guest to eat Chiao Tze, it is important for the guest to bring a healthy appetite. It was not uncommon for a person to be expected to eat fifty or more pieces, otherwise the host might be offended." Immediately I turned to Mrs. Sheng and asked for her forgiveness, "I know that under these rules I will not be able to accomplish such a spectacular feat and do not want to cause you any loss of face." The Shengs all laughed at my expressed predicament, and Mr. Sheng accepted my apology saying, "You will not be expected on this occasion, but perhaps sometime in the future, when Chioa Tze is the only course being served at a meal, you can achieve this mark of distinction."

For our next course, a large soup tureen was brought to the center of the table in which I could see a large ring of black meat. Mr. Sheng's eyes grew big as he watched Mrs. Sheng begin to serve this delicacy. He told me that this was one of their most popular dishes, eel soup. He explained, "This dish is prepared specifically to stimulate the male virility." So, he cautioned me—in good humor—"Be careful as to how much you consume." He went on to say, "This food was often served in the old days to the master of the house as he prepared himself mentally and physically for the attentions of his concubines." "In old China," he continued, "it was a custom that a man of position should take more than one woman, depending upon his status of wealth, into his house. Families of low classes considered it an honor to commit their daughters to a man of higher station so that she could improve upon her education and culture, while at the same time offering physical and social attention to her master. Those who truly found the source of his pleasures were usually rewarded very handsomely . . . of course, the obligation of the concubine then being to share the rewards with her family." Understanding that Mr. Sheng expressed a great degree of loyalty to this social convention, I asked very subtly, "How does one who maintains concubines find a wife to accept and understand this relationship?" He answered that there is an old Chinese saying, "A wife is married for her virtues and the concubine sought for her beauty." "The Chinese wife assumes a position of family dominance and authority over the concubines . . . and every Chinese girl is brought up with an understanding and acceptance of this relationship." Jennifer very subtly interjected, "Baba, every girl was!" Mrs. Sheng drew Mr. Sheng's glare at this contradiction in her direction as she explained, "Although this system was common in old China, from a woman's viewpoint it was extremely difficult to accept, especially when one or more concubines took a position of favor with the master." Almost as if expecting that I enjoyed the same relationship, Mr. Sheng proceeded to ask, "Would you be interested in taking another woman into your family as a concubine?" This question was translated with some difficulty by Tien Lai and also caused shades of embarrassment on the part of the children. I attempted to answer the question in all honesty by saying, "I'm sure that most Western men would enjoy the thought of maintaining a harem . . . as we call this convention in our

Western society . . . but it is not accepted as a social norm within the Christian religion. More important, most men, even though they might have sufficient wealth to support this luxury, would find it difficult in our society to cope with more than one." Mr. Sheng smiled broadly at my response, and with a certain amount of pride exclaimed, "And so we find a fundamental difference in our two cultures!" For the first time in the evening, the children, first Linda, who was married, expressed their feelings on this subject. Politely, she said, "Father, we children recognize that the practice of concubinage was common in your generation, which was representative of old China. I speak my true feelings when I say that I, of the new generation and new China, cannot accept this family philosophy. Our new generation believes that the relationship between a man and a woman is one which is made out of love for each other. Two people truly in love cannot accept the presence of a third person in this partnership." Mr. Sheng took exception to his daughter's feelings and expressed himself with almost a feeling of anger. "How can two young people recognize what is love, when there is really no definition to this word in our language? Two young people . . . like yourself and Paul, your husband . . . are almost as if deaf, dumb, and blind because of your physical attraction to each other. There is much more to a marriage than the physical relationship. This is the reason for our practice of matchmaking. It is only through the eyes, ears, and a sense of touch that your parents can see your strengths and weaknesses and clearly . . . without sacrifice to judgment . . . Accept the matchmaker, to find a person who will bring to this union of two people . . . complementary qualities." Tien Lai entered the conversation for the first time by saying, "Father, there is much truth to what you say. But children, like ourselves, are exposed to more education and see more of the world around us, and I feel that we grow in our ability to make a rational judgment about selection of a mate on our own." "Ah, yes," retorted his father, "but still you young people seek out the matchmaker to get confirmation that you are right for each other, which in itself is an admission of your shortcomings." Almost in reverence, Mr. Sheng concluded the family conversation saying,

"It is easy to govern a kingdom, but difficult to control one's family."

As the next dish of minced squab was served, Mr. Sheng spoke quietly to me, with the benefit to Tien Lai's translation that he would like to speak further to me on this subject of the concubine, later in the evening. I acknowledged his invitation with pleasure, as Mrs. Sheng then began to show me how to fix this most delicious delicacy. She placed a very thin pancake on my plate and then garnished it with a little doily-shaped piece of lettuce, a soy-based sauce, and small shoots of green onion. Finally, she covered the pancake with pieces of finely diced meat. I didn't know quite what to expect, as I translated in my mind that squab was really pigeon in our country, but as I rolled this pancake and took my first taste of it, my fears of unknown tastes quickly disappeared. "Mrs. Sheng," I exclaimed, "this dish is truly a superb treat to the taste buds." She humbly accepted my compliment and proceeded to make me a second, which I enjoyed equally as much as the first.

Almost as if an apology, Mr. Sheng initiated the conversation again, admitting that there is one shortcoming to the practice of concubines. He proceeded to tell a story about a modern general. "We have a general . . . named Ho . . . still living and very healthy at the age of eighty-eight. So the story goes, General Ho has taken a new concubine into his family at the rate of one each year and now boasts of an entourage of some seventy females, who have produced more than two hundred grandchildren . . . the exact number being somewhat unofficial. General Ho is a very prominent figure within military circles, and as such is frequently called upon to represent the government at community activities. It is said that one day while at a sporting event to present ribbons and medals to the winners, he began talking to a young eighteen-year-old boy who had won the hundred-meter dash. Upon congratulating him, the general asked who the boy's father was. The boy looked at the general straight in the eye and said, 'Why, sir? You are.' Undaunted, the general put his arm around the boy and said, 'Congratulations, my son . . . what is your name?'"

As typical of most Chinese meals, when one approaches the feeling of being full, you can expect at least two more dishes will remain to be consumed, and as I viewed the sight of the steamed crab claws, I knew that I would force myself to enjoy this dish as much as I had enjoyed the others. The claws had been cracked, and all that remained was to extract the sweet meat from the shell. Mrs. Sheng then demonstrated that the meat was to be dipped into a sauce of soy and vinegar, which had been amply garnished with ginger. Once again, the taste of this typical Shanghainese seafood dish was superb. "My son tells me that you are about to start a business in our country. May I ask you the name of your business and its nature?" Proudly, I answered, "Mr. Sheng, it is my task, which I look forward to with great anticipation, to establish a company which we will call ABC, Ltd. Our products will be in the consumer electronics market. We plan to start producing radios and tape recorders, and later stereo hi-fi equipment." Mr. Sheng responded, "What, may I ask the definition of your company's name, ABC?" To which I replied, "It may sound a little corny, but it stands for 'A Business in China.'" Mr. Sheng pondered my explanation with a very learned look and then said, "May I also suggest that in our country, it might also stand for 'Always Be Calm.' Patience is a virtue to the Chinese, and 'if you are not patient in small things, you will bring great plans to naught.' I see in you many qualities which will help you build a fine and successful business. But one more question I should ask. How many American managers will you bring to our country to help you manage?" My reply was simply, "Mr. Sheng, I am the only American. It is my plan that all of the executive level positions be filled by Chinese and hopefully among them, we will find one who has the capability to become the Lao Ban when my job has been finished." He received my comments with pleasure and once again offered a toast of success.

From my prior exposure at the Chinese dinner table, I knew that this last dish of fresh fruit was, in fact, to be the last. I didn't realize that time had gone so quickly, but glancing at my watch, I saw that it was now after eleven o'clock and so I began my apologies as to my need to depart. "I must get back to the hotel and pack my suitcase for my departure for tomorrow morning." After thanking Mrs. Sheng for the delightful evening, I found Mr. Sheng . . . along with Tien Lai . . . taking me to a corner of the living room to have a secretive conversation apart from the rest of the family. Very seriously he looked straight into my eyes and said, "Mr. Tai Le, I have enjoyed the opportunity of having you in our home, and I do hope that you will once again feel free to join us when you return to our country with your family. Although I am from the old school of thinking and you are from the new, I would like to ask for your permission to consider a very weighty proposal. I would like to ask you to consider entering a gentlemen's agreement . . . since a contract is no longer legal . . . to accept my daughter, Jennifer, into your home. In this way, I look forward to bridging the gap between our cultures . . . hoping that it might help you understand our philosophy and we, in turn, better understand yours." Realizing that his offer was made in all sincerity, I qualified my answer saying, "Mr. Sheng, I respect very much the gracious request which you have made, and I am prepared to accept, with your understanding of one Western condition. Your daughter is welcome in our household . . . not as a concubine, but as a friend and as a token of my esteem for your family. Jennifer is welcome in our house as if she were a daughter. I know my wife will be happy to develop that relationship with the objective that perhaps she can learn in living with our family more about our ways." Proudly he expressed, "I understand your condition and I would like to seal our agreement with your handshake."

Tien Lai and the twins, Jennifer and Linda, all volunteered to accompany me back to the hotel. It was an opportune time for me to rely upon Tien Lai to help explain this new family pact to Jennifer. Surprisingly, she expressed delight in having the opportunity to live with and become part of an American family, saying that she looked forward very much to meeting my wife and children and sharing the hospitality of our home when we returned in August. I purposely said good-bye to the three of them at the front door to the hotel. Despite my expressed feelings that they need not feel obligated to be a part of my bon voyage party at the airport tomorrow, they all insisted.

Wanting to spend a few minutes to reflect upon my decision, I decided to venture to the Champagne room on the twelfth floor of the hotel to sip a scotch and water as I surveyed the glittering lights of the city below. A dance band played a wide range of rock and roll, as well as sentimental music, to a dance floor full of couples ... most of them whom were the typical Oriental father and daughter combinations. I chuckled to myself to think that here I am ... an Occidental ... with a similar father-daughter relationship within my own family ... although knowing full well that this one would be above board and not exercised in the clandestine environment of one of the local hotel rooms. An hour must have slipped by as I sat enjoying my reverie, when I was surprised to see an elderly gentleman with a young and quite beautiful companion standing beside my table. Much to my chagrin, I found Mr. Sheng, my host of earlier in the evening, introducing me to a young lady, who obviously wasn't his wife or one of his daughters. Mr. Sheng proudly introduced me to his "Mei Ling." A little embarrassed, I regained my composure and offered for both of them to join me at my table. As Mei Ling translated in her broken English, Mr. Sheng made no pretenses about the relationship which existed between him and Mei Ling and openly described to her the extent of the friendship and family relationship that existed between us. Just as quickly as they came, they disappeared out onto the dance floor. It was a rather amusing sight to see this very distinguished sixty-year-old man dancing to a modified rock and roll with his mistress, a concubine in every sense of the word. After finishing my drink and finding that it was now one o'clock in the morning and remembering that I had an appointment to keep at eight, I wandered by the dance floor and expressed my apologies for leaving Mr. Sheng and his companion and said my "Dzai jens" and returned to my room.

I can honestly say that it was somewhat difficult to straighten out all of the pieces of this Chinese jigsaw puzzle in my mind ... concerning the events of the evening. One certainly couldn't come to the conclusion that life was going to be dull.

Chapter 20

Mission Accomplished

My last morning came too early with my wake-up call at 6:30 a.m. The satisfaction of the first seven days was dampened as I looked out my window to find it raining. "Looks like a good morning to sleep in," I thought to myself, but I knew I could not afford that luxury, much remained to be done before my plane left at 11:50 a.m. The thought of meeting and starting out my day with Rita was a positive stimulus to motivating me to shave, shower, dress, and pack my luggage before going to the coffee shop for breakfast.

As I left the room, I was greeted by my favorite floor boy Walter. He volunteered, "Tai Le Hsien Sheng, you leave today?" "Yes?" "Can I help you?" "Yes, Walter, today is the day. I would appreciate your help when I check out after breakfast, OK?" "OK," he echoed, as I entered the elevator. Upon my exit into the lobby, the ever-present elevator starter was there to greet me with her usual, "Dzao An, ni hao?" It even appeared as if the coffee shop, normally in its wake-up routine at seven o'clock, was way ahead of schedule today as the head waitress was waiting for me, with a big smile and a "Good morning, Mr. Tai Le." She promptly seated me almost as if I were a special guest of honor. The dreariness of this rainy day and the early hour were but a mood of the past as I realized how much at home I felt with these Chinese people. As I savored my fresh fruit plate of cantaloupe, papaya, pineapple, bananas, and watermelon, a thought came to me. I had to tell it to someone as I left the coffee shop, so I stopped to tell it to the head waitress. "You know, I've only been here eight days. I'm leaving to go back to the United States, but I want to let you know and tell the others, I've enjoyed my visit, meeting you people, and believe it or not, I can't wait to come back." I know she didn't understand what prompted my outpouring of emotion, but she did have sympathy for my words, and with a broad smile of satisfaction, she posed a question, "Tai Le Hsien Sheng, you can come back. Hao bu hao?" Returning her smile, I said, "Hao." And with that I expressed my thanks by giving her a tip of RMB$100 and turned to leave, saying, "Hsieh Hsieh Nimen." She caught me in the lobby and pressed the RMB$100 tip into my hand, glanced quickly at my face, then looked down, and spoke softly, "No, no, such a tip is not necessary. Your thanks and happiness is your and our gift."

When I returned to my room, I found that Walter had everything ready for me to go. Taking care of last-minute details, brushing my teeth, and while doing my duty, the realization of what true culture really was hit me like a ton of bricks. As I reeled off four squares of toilet paper, I laughed out loud 'till my stomach hurt. I had been in China eight days, gone to the men's room in countless places, and awoke to the fact that not in one place, bars, restaurants, offices, dance halls, or any other place had I found any toilet paper that wasn't two-ply and "white cloud" soft. I couldn't help but say it out loud to Walter as I left my room. "Walter, you Chinese really have culture." It's too bad he couldn't appreciate my analogy. Just then, he spoke, finding it difficult to put together the right words, but it was easy to read the pride in his feelings. "Tai Le Hsien Sheng, I think you not well for two to three days, but then I find you have some first-class girls to visit you. Now I know you No. 1 man. You like our Country. We like you come back, OK?" "Hao," I replied, "I will come back . . . in two more months." "Good!" he exclaimed. "You ask for room on my floor, hao bu hao?" "Hao," I acknowledged and pressed two RMB$100 bills into his hand with a handshake. As he followed me into the elevator with my luggage, he looked at me almost as if with a guilty conscience and said, "My service not worth RMB$200 this time, but I keep and next time I do a double first-class job for you."

Patty Chen, my favorite room clerk, was on duty and smiled as I handed her my keys and said, "Patty, will you help me check out and do me one last favor?" "Yes, Tai Le Hsien Sheng, I will help you, but if you check out, then I will have no one to help in the future." When I told her, "I will be back in two months," and asked her, "Please, can you make reservations for me and my family in August," her look of sadness turned to one of pleasure. "You come back soon, we will look forward to seeing you again and meet your tai-tai (wife) and shiao haidze (children)." Pushing a reservation card in front of me, she promised, "You fill out this card, I make room for you, junda."

As I paid my bills of RMB$1200 (US$150), I teased her, "Patty, can you do me one last favor? Give me directions, in Chinese, to get to the Tai Fong Bank on Shanghai South Road?" "OK," she said, "but this is the last time. From now on you must find your own way." As I extended my hand to say thanks, she explained in a very serious manner, "Tai Le Hsien Sheng, hotel people all like you, so you must promise to come back." "I promise," and with that I hooked her little finger, and she looked at me coyly saying, "You know, you are almost Chinese." With that we both exchanged "Dzai Jens," and I exited the door to catch a taxi, my little paper slip with Chinese directions in my hand.

The doorman added one more little distinct courtesy as he held the umbrella over my head while I got into the cab, and he loaded the luggage into the front seat. By now, I thought, I'd have the knack of getting into the cab without difficulty, but as was my habit, I did a creditable job of bumping all my limbs before getting settled. I guess I really didn't notice the rain or the usual idiotic driving habits as I began to reflect on my experiences of these first eight days, and before I realized it, we had pulled up to the entrance to the bank. My reverie was rudely awakened as I got out of the taxi into the pouring rain, paid the driver the shameful sum of RMB$5 (US$.70) for my twenty-minute joy ride, took my luggage out of the cab, and sloshed down the alley to the side entrance of ABC's new Taipei executive suite. My spirits were somewhat dampened as I squished my way back up the backstairs and entered the office, thinking out loud, "How are we going to do any work? There are no chairs, no desks." Just then, I realized that my Jane Armstrong, Girl Friday, Beauty Like Music, Rita, was one step ahead of me. Somehow, she had acquired from the bank one desk and two chairs. As she greeted me with a pleasant "Dzao" and a polite giggle at my drowned-rat appearance, I grumbled, "Why does a pleasant trip have to end with a day like today?" She promptly steered me to the restroom facilities, which it was apparent would be shared by both male and female, helped me take off my coat, handed me a towel to dry myself off, and said, "Tai Le Hsien Sheng, you shouldn't be discouraged by the weather. Rain is a good omen to Chinese businessmen. Water is like profit. It starts with a little stream and gets deeper and wider the longer it flows. Hao bu hao?"

"You're right," I said, "again, as usual." And with that, I felt myself break into a broad smile and a very pleasant sense of satisfaction came over me. "Rita," I remarked, "with a philosophy like that and people like you, ABC is going to be like a typhoon of success." She acknowledged my play on words, and then with all seriousness, she said, "Time is a most precious commodity, not to be wasted today. We should begin to work, hao bu hao?" She was absolutely right, so we both turned to walk back into the office, and without lost motion began to discuss the myriad of items to be accomplished during my absence.

She took notes, in shorthand as I talked, and asked questions and commented when she didn't understand, and/or wanted to add a thought for our consideration. Establishing priority list, I started, "The first order of business is to get the offices partitioned, decorated, and furnished." As I proceeded to detail each step to be accomplished, she looked at me with her face full of confidence and said, "Mr. Tai Le, I think I understand what you want. Please leave the details to me. I know a good office furniture maker who is reasonable. First let me excuse myself, find a telephone to call a friend of mine who is a contractor, and get him to come here right away to talk about the office remodeling. His name is Chen." With that, she disappeared, and within two minutes, she was back saying, "He will be here within twenty minutes." Pausing to let the effect of her efficiency sink in, she then quietly picked up her shorthand book and waited for me to resume my instructions.

Collecting my thoughts, I began to itemize, "Rita, I'd like to have you take care of the following:

1. Get some ABC Ltd. letterhead stationery and envelopes printed.
2. Order two secretarial desks and five executive-type desks.
3. Place an order for one IBM typewriter for yourself.
4. Draft a board resolution to open up checking account and time deposit accounts with the Tai Fong branch bank here. Work with Mr. Wu, the manager. Send them to me in the United States for signature, and I will return them.
5. Open up a personal checking account for me with the bank here.
6. Then, I'd like to have you work with Henry Chao to develop a proposed list of architects for me to interview when I return in August to develop the plans for the building of our factory.
7. Keep after Henry on the status of our FIA status, and if you have to, to keep things moving within the government, call on Minister Tseng. You should know him (I winked at her) since he was one of your references.
8. Next, make an application for a telex installation for our plant.
9. We'll also need a local P.O. box for our mail.
10. Our stateside auditors have suggested the firm of H. Y. Sung here as our local audit firm. Get with their senior partner and ask him to help you set up a set of accounting records.
11. How about getting some ABC office signs installed at the street and in the alley at the entrance?"

Well, I proceeded to list a total of thirty-seven items that she could work on in my absence, and much to my amazement, she didn't flinch, and there wasn't a single item she felt she would have difficulty accomplishing.

About the time we finished, there was a knock on the door, and Rita promptly proceeded to let Mr. Chen in, and after a few words of Chinese, she introduced this tall, thin man with a crew cut and a smile that radiated with friendship and the gold of dental care.

I apologized, saying, "I'm sorry I don't have more time to get acquainted, my flight leaves for the United States in two hours, so please excuse me if I seem to hurry our conversation." "Mr. Tai Le," he replied with obvious understanding, "I, Johnny Chen, will do first-class work for you. You tell me . . . I will do." So, I explained, "I'll need to have partitions to make two private offices." He nodded as I showed him about where and how big I wanted the offices. "Then, I'd like some reverse-cycle heating and air-conditioning units, adequate to heat and cool these rooms when we have about twenty people on board." "Hao," he acknowledged, simply. "I'd also like to have you get some window drapes installed and then give the whole place a nice pleasant coat of pastel green paint, to match our loge colors." Again, he signaled his willingness with a nod of his head.

"Now, Mr. Chen," I asked, "can you give me an estimate of the cost?" Quickly, he began the rough calculations in his head, and within two minutes, he quoted, "Tai Le Hsien Sheng, all this work will cost you RMB$12,000 (US$1500.) Air-conditioners, we maybe need three, new they cost RMB$24,000 (US$3,000.) Very expensive. Used, maybe the total is RMB$8,000 (US$1,000)." Seeing my pained look at the price of the new units, he hastened to add, "You buy used ones. I will guarantee, if they don't work, anytime I will repair—no charge, OK?"

Looking at Rita for her thoughts, she answered my quizzical look saying, "Mr. Tai Le, Chen Hsien Sheng has a very good reputation. I will vouch for his workmanship and honesty." With that assurance, I shook hands with Mr. Chen and said, "OK, let's use the used equipment. When you have finished the work, Miss Chu will pay you by check. Hao bu hao?" Mr. Chen beamed with the award of this small job, and with a vigorous handshake, profusely thanked me in both English and Chinese, and then speaking a few words to Rita in Chinese, he departed.

Looking at her watch, Miss Chu began to close up shop and said, "Mr. Tai Le, we had best get ready to go to the airport. It takes about a half hour and you should be there to check in about one hour before flight time."

"OK," I say, "let's go." "May I accompany you?" she asked rather shyly. "I would like to go over my assignments to make sure I have everything clear in my mind."

Saying a quick good-bye to Mr. Wu, to thank him and to advise him of my plans to return in two months, we exited the front door of the bank to hail a cab on this busy, hustle-bustle street, which was soaked from the pouring rain. Rita attracted a cab within seconds, and we piled in. She giggled as she watched me bump my head, my knees, and she said, "Our Datsun Bluebird is not a very good car for you, but I'm sorry. It is all we have for taxis here in Taipei." "Don't worry," I replied, "I'll get used to them."

As we sped toward the airport, she repeated from memory, with perfection, the list of things she was going to be responsible to accomplish during my absence. "I hope I'm not asking too much of you," I queried. "No, Mr. Tai Le," she said confidently, "please don't you worry. I will be all right."

After sitting for a few minutes in silence, I felt the need and impulse to say, "Rita, you know I have every confidence in you." As the words came out, she placed her hand on mine, almost with the same effect I feel when I put my hand on my son's shoulder.

By the time we reached the airport, the rain had stopped, but the sky was still overcast and the streets still glistened of wetness. The airport, even in this dreary atmosphere, was a striking example of the blend of the old and the new in this country. Its graceful tile roof, pagoda style canopies, and swept up roofline blended well with its contemporary architecture and facility conveniences. The building gave the traveler a pleasant first and last impression.

As we entered the busy lobby of the departure area of the building, I was greeted with my own "going away" party, Tien Lai and the twins in their airline stewardess uniforms. Jennifer and Linda both placed leis of flowers around my neck, and Jennifer, with a radiant smile, whispered softly, almost in jest, "Father, I wish you a safe journey, and I will wait anxiously for your return."

As had been indicated by the reference to Tien Lai on Rita's resume, it was apparent that they were the best of friends. They walked toward the China Airlines ticket counter to help get me checked in, while I walked up to the dining room with Linda and Jennifer, one on each side of me. It made a middle-aged man feel young to be in the company of these two absolutely beautiful women. "I want you both to know," I remarked, "that I'm enjoying with pleasure my last hours as a bachelor in China. You know, I only wish my twin brother could see me now . . ." The girls both looked up at me and said, "Hsieh Hsieh Ni." Then, in all seriousness, I continued, as we found a table and sat down, waiting for Tien Lai and Rita to join us, "You know, the next time I am here, I'll be a father of a family. Makes a young man of thirty-five feel old."

Just then, Rita and Tien Lai joined us, with the consoling but sad warning from Tien Lai, "Well, all is OK. Your flight is boarding in about twenty minutes."

Knowing that time was running out, I attempted to express my feelings of appreciation for their friendships, their commitment to assist me in my new business venture, and the hospitality of their family, but somehow the words didn't seem to be adequate to describe the feeling within me. As we sipped our cokes, I made one last attempt before we rose to go to the customs clearance gate. "I know that it is probably not appropriate to use the word 'love' in Chinese, but I have this feeling that I cannot describe in any other word in English. I have fallen in 'love' with your country, your people, and you . . . all as friends. I know that is not proper to be impatient in China, but I cannot wait to return, so our relationships can be continued, so please be patient with my impatience."

With that, we all walked together to the gate, and as quickly as I had arrived, I was departing. The usual rush of confusion took place, and my passport was stamped, my shot records checked, and my hand luggage as cleared, and then we were finally taken as a group by bus out to our waiting China Airlines 707 bound for Honolulu and San Francisco.

It wasn't 'till I was on my way up the gangway that I had a chance to look around. There, on the mezzanine, I saw my faithful friends and new employee all waving good-bye. I could read their lips saying, "Dzai Jen." The literal translation of the phrase came to mind, "see you again," almost poetical when I remembered that the Chinese don't have a word for good-bye. Optimistically, they expect to see their friends again. Returning their farewell, I entered the plane to look for a seat. It wasn't till I sat down and buckled up, then hearing the crew close the hatch and prepare to start the engines for our taxi to takeoff that the real feeling of pleasure, as well as sadness began to overcome my emotional equilibrium. I had a large lump in my throat as the plane lifted off the runway. Looking out the window, I could see the pilot heading for a clear blue sky window in the clouds, and as the plane entered the cloud formation, my last glance at the ground gave me a look over the beautiful, terraced rice paddies, their water glistening in the sunlight. As they blended into the mountain tops and the island departed from view, my "grass roots" from the West blended in with my love for the "bamboo shoots" of the East. With a great feeling of satisfaction, I realized that I had just built my bridge between two worlds . . . two cultures . . . separated by an ocean . . . halfway around the world from each other . . . now ONE in my heart.

www.ingramcontent.com/pod-product-compliance
Lightning Source LLC
Chambersburg PA
CBHW030942180526
45163CB00002B/678